D1117002

design for play

design for play

Richard Dattner AIA

VNR **Van Nostrand Reinhold Company**
New York   Cincinnati   Toronto   London   Melbourne

To my mother and father

Van Nostrand Reinhold Company Regional Offices:
New York Cincinnati Chicago Millbrae Dallas

Van Nostrand Reinhold Company Foreign Offices:
London Toronto Melbourne

Copyright © 1969 by Reinhold Book Corporation
Library of Congress Catalog Card No. 69-16380

All rights reserved. No part of this work covered by the copyrights hereon may be reproduced or used in any form or by any means — graphic, electronic, or mechanical, including photocopying, recording, taping, or information storage and retrieval systems — without written permission of the publisher. Manufactured in the United States of America

Designed by Edward Marson
Printed by Halliday Lithograph Company
Bound by A. Horowitz & Son

Published by Van Nostrand Reinhold Company
450 West 33rd Street, New York, N.Y. 10001

Published simultaneously in Canada by
D. Van Nostrand Company (Canada), Ltd.

16 15 14 13 12 11 10 9 8 7 6 5 4 3 2 1

contents

the philosophy of play 1

Man only plays when he is human in the full sense of the word, and he is only completely human when he is playing.

— Friedrich Schiller

We can best understand what play is if we think of it as the opposite of work — the two terms to a large extent define each other. The difference between work and play is not always obvious from an examination of the activity but has to do, rather, with the mode of acting, or the reason for which the activity is performed. Thus, although a tennis player and a laborer may be expending similar amounts of effort, perspiration, and concentration, we immediately understand that the tennis player is playing, while the laborer is working. The activities are being performed for very different reasons.

The activities of children of a certain age are very much like those of some adults: the children act like firemen or soldiers or airplane pilots or nurses, yet we have no question about what these children are doing — they are at play. In the same way, some adult activities bear a striking resemblance to those of children. Television presents a daily spectacle of adults making grotesque faces, throwing pies at each other, and falling down in a variety of ways to the accompaniment of laughter. But neither we nor the performers are for one minute deceived — this is work, and of the most difficult kind.

"To climb adds unused dimensions to the awareness of our body. Play here gives a sense of divine leeway, of excess space." — Erik H. Erikson

This not to say that work and play never overlap or coexist; the motivation behind any activity is complex, and often contains elements of work and play. For our purposes, however, it is useful to emphasize the unique qualities of each, so that we can form a clear picture of what conditions are essential or desirable for play.

Work is necessary. We work because we have to — to earn a living, to secure the necessities and luxuries of life, to provide for ourselves and our families. Work is, to some extent, not voluntary. Even those of us who find satisfaction in our work are not insensitive to the temptations of a warm spring day or a warm winter bed: we leave both against our wishes. Work is an adult undertaking, implying an acceptance of our responsibility to others and the placing of this responsibility above our personal desires in many instances. Without our commitment to our work, and through it to the society in which we live, the complex interrelationships by which our world operates would quickly break down. The fact that work is necessary should not be taken to mean it is necessarily unpleasant. Much work is unpleasant and demeaning, but that is an unfortunate

result of our industrial and social environment and not of the nature of work. It is possible to foresee a time when stultifying, repetitious, and otherwise undesirable tasks will be performed by machines whose very nature suits them well for precisely those occupations that are a form of living death for human beings. All work will not disappear, however, for work is not only necessary to maintain and further our collective life, but is vital in giving shape, meaning, and purpose to each person's life.

Work can be forced, but play, like love, is a supremely voluntary undertaking. Play can occur only in a condition of freedom, because it is above all doing what you want to do, when and where you want to do it. As work is a response to external pressures, play is a manifestation of internal needs and wishes. Like work, it is a necessity, but one we require of ourselves to maintain a healthy balance and perspective in our lives. All work and no play not only makes Jack a dull boy but deprives him of that full expression of personal freedom which makes him uniquely human. This sense of play is expressed in a number of the accepted definitions of the word "play"; i.e., exercise or action for amusement; freedom,

Adventure Playground: London (Camden)

The results of play, unlike those of work, cannot be classified, measured, counted, or sold.

Vacant Lot: New York City

Play is scope for action.

Play is doing what you want to do, when you want to do it.

room, or scope for motion or action; freedom or abstinence from work, etc.

Adult play usually takes the form of recreation — literally, re-creation of our selves after periods of work by engaging in freely chosen activities that restore our sense of completeness. It may vary from the most strenuous competitive sports to the most sedentary games, but all recreation is doing what we want to do at a particular time.

A form of adult play less common than recreation and more closely resembling the play of children is creative expression — art and science. Mathematicians "play" with numbers, painters and sculptors "play" with forms, and composers "play" with sounds. The literature written about and by creative persons is full of references to the play element in all forms of creativity, and many parallels may be drawn between play and the act of creation.

Work is concerned with production: we work to produce, and the object we make or service we perform gives our work its name. The value of work is measured by the quality, quantity, or importance of the product, and all other considerations are secondary. The results of work can be classified, measured, counted, and sold. Work may be rewarded by pleasure and the pride of accomplishment, but for most people, it is done as means of securing wealth, prestige, power, fame. It is impossible to "do" play — it is an end in itself and, like virtue, is its own reward. It is the process of play, not the product, that gives us satisfaction. This is not to say that play is never concerned with results: all play is in some way concerned with the achievement of goals, even when these aims are not consciously stated by the player. But whether the goal is the winning of a game for an adult, or an infant's mastery, after repeated attempts, of the way to jiggle a mobile above his crib, it is the process of mastering that is important, and this process cannot be measured, counted, or sold. A child who spends hours building a sand castle at the edge of the sea is not so interested in the end result as he is in the making of it. He would not be so caught up in an identical castle made for him by an adult. He may, just a moment after he completes the final turret, either completely demolish his masterpiece or simply walk away from it. But he knows something that we have forgotten to remember: the sea, or time, will

Fire Hydrant: New York City

Play cannot be "done" — it is an end in itself.

". . . In trifling, in dallying, we lazily thumb our noses at time, our slave driver." — Erik H. Erikson

Rooftop Playground: New York City

Play, like virtue, is its own reward.

Central Park: New York City

The child who plays with real sticks and leaves transforms them in his imagination into whatever he wants.

Street Play: New York City

All play is concerned with the achievement of goals, but it is the process of achieving that is important.

always take his castles from him, but the acts of building, destroying, or walking away from them will forever be his. Even the juvenile delinquent knows this, although he does not comprehend it. Crime, vandalism, and destruction are the obverse of creation. Those who cannot create will destroy, for the same reason the architect of the sand castle destroys — to experience life as a process, to have acted.

Work occurs within a set of rules and conditions imposed externally by a system that is a product of the complex balance of countless persons, institutions, traditions, laws of economics, and social mores. In a free society we may attempt to modify the rules or replace them, but we can never control them completely and absolutely. Unless we are revolutionaries, we work within a matrix of choices we may find partially unacceptable, and if we are revolutionaries, we still face the necessity of replacing this framework of allowable behavior with one of our own creation. In either case the rules are externally imposed.

Play — that of adults as well as that of children — also takes place within a framework of rules, often very intricate ones. Our national sport of

football is virtually incomprehensible to a foreigner until the involved regulations covering every imaginable situation are explained, even as rugby and cricket are a mystery to most of us. Children create an equally strict order in their play. The child whose game requires that the space under the kitchen table be a fort under attack by Apache warriors always has the option, if things get too hot, of changing the rules to save his scalp. He invented the rules, and he can cancel them if he wants to. If his play involves other children, and they resist a modification of the rules, the ultimate decision is still available — he can decide that he no longer wants to play.

The important distinction between the rules governing work and those governing play is that the latter are self-imposed. Either by design or by choice, the rules of play are internal rules. Adult games are usually more intractable and are often controlled by rules of long standing, not open to modification. But the players freely choose to play within them and are equally free to stop playing. (This does not hold for professional "players" whose participation is really work. They are concerned with the production of games won, making a living,

Play is not bound by reality — it leaves the everyday world far behind.

and so on. The last thing professional athletics is, is play.)

Work, finally, is performed in the real world. Real things are produced, sold, counted, and moved. Reality demands compromises, accommodations, and modifications, and constantly challenges our ingenuity — it is always imperfect. Work, like politics, occurs within the realm of the possible. It is the challenge of dealing with reality that makes work exciting, and meeting the challenge that gives us satisfaction. Play is not bound by reality — it is extraordinary. The untrammeled character of play is reflected in our language: we play with words, we entertain playful thoughts, our imagination plays, we go to plays — always leaving far behind the everyday, real world.

The child who plays with real sticks and leaves transforms them in his imagination into whatever he wants and creates another, more personal, reality not bounded by the real and commonplace. In this respect play is similar to magic, and it is not surprising that both children and primitive societies are much influenced by magical thinking, for in play the normal rules of cause and effect are suspended.

Play is the expression of human freedom.

A sense of secrecy often permeates play: for example, children delight in secrets and special hiding places. The place where children play is a sort of magic circle, outside and separate from the rest of the world; it has its own time, which cannot be measured by our clocks. Within this all is transformed and controlled by imagination, and a perfect world is possible.

It is in play that our desire for a perfect world under our complete control is satisfied, and it is there that all the meanings of play meet: the theatrical play that can take us out of the real world into another world born of imagination and illusion (the word "illusion," from *in ludere,* literally means in play); play as a spontaneous activity occurring within freely chosen limits; play as a process or a way of acting; play as a manifestation of choice. This is what Schiller meant when he wrote that man is only completely human when he is playing, for play is the expression of human freedom, and, in a large sense, play is freedom.

Street Play: Heidelberg

Some aspects of play are universal.

the social function of play

2

*Train up a child in the way he should go: and
when he is old he will not depart from it.*

— Proverbs 22:6

For many years, children's play was thought to be little more than an expression of excess energy and good spirits, an activity that adults should indulge so that children would be better able to do serious work at home and at school. Their activities were not considered important, except as they impinged on the adult world; children, the saying went, should be seen and not heard. The writings of Freud and, subsequently, studies of child-rearing practices in a variety of cultures established the importance of childhood experience in the development of the adult personality and demonstrated that play is a major component of that experience. Although the play of infants is strikingly similar irrespective of the culture in which it occurs, adults soon begin to stress those aspects of children's activity that most closely reflect the values of the adult society.

Control of children's play is one way in which a society prepares the child to participate eventually in the world of adults. To a large extent the process of transmitting the values of a culture is unconscious, and no distinction is made between the positive values that are being handed down and the negative characteristics which every culture inherits. In gen-

eral, most of us simply accept what is taught us, and pass it on to our children as a package, the good with the bad.

A brief example will serve to illustrate the differences in allowable patterns of play in two countries, and the extent to which play both expresses the social values of a culture and conditions children to accept them. The following observations are taken from *Childhood in Contemporary Cultures* by Margaret Mead and Martha Wolfenstein, and supplemented by my own experiences.

It is customary for Parisian children to be taken to a park regularly by an adult — parent, nurse, or grandparent. There are few playgrounds in our sense of the word: the few communal facilities of swings and carrousels charge admission and require parents to accompany their children, yet the parks are full of playing children. The usual procedure is for the adult to find a spot on one of the innumerable park benches, while the child plays directly in front of him, very often with the sand mixture of the path. This play is different from the play of an American child in a number of significant ways, a few of which are noted here.

The distinctions of what toy belongs to whom are strictly maintained by the adult in France. For example, if little Pierre playfully picks up a sand pail that belongs to a boy playing nearby, Pierre's mother will immediately take it away from him, scold him, and offer apologies to the mother of the neighboring boy. Toys are regarded as the property of the parents, and the adults keep a close watch to see that no mixing of property takes place. Contrast this with a similar situation in the United States. Typically, the parents of the two youngsters would urge them to share their toys with their playmates, and would be upset if they refused to share.

The French concern for what is theirs is reflected, also, in the fact that their children seldom play with children outside the family. Thus, siblings will play together even when they are separated in age by a few years rather than play with contemporaries from another family. I once observed a boy and girl about two years old playing near each other in a sandbox. After a while the girl expressed some interest in the boy and began to help him with his sand construction. Immediately, both mothers got up and separated the children. The mothers then resumed their places on the

Children's Zoo: Rapperswil (Zurich)

Adult influence on play is one way in which a society
transmits its values and prepares children to participate
in the adult world.

Carrousel: Paris

The way that children play reflects the way their culture feels about children. French children are sedate and prefer to play alone, though in the company of others.

Street Play: New York City

American children are active and gregarious. Americans regard childhood as an ideal time of life.

bench without a word, and the children resumed their solitary, albeit adjacent, play. In such ways is the solidarity of the French family created.

As friendly contact is discouraged between playing children in France, so is any expression of even the mildest aggression. If one child hits another, both parents immediately intervene. The victim of the attack, rather than fighting back, will look to the adults to get him out of the situation, and the aggressor is usually subjected to a verbal tirade from both. Absent here are the American concepts of standing up for one's own rights and the right to defend oneself in a fair fight. The lesson is, rather, that any form of physical aggression is prohibited.

This prohibition encompasses all kinds of strenuous activity, and French parents are constantly admonishing their children to refrain from boisterous behavior with cries of *"Doucement, doucement!"* ("Gently, gently!") Thus, French children are considerably less physically active than their American counterparts, usually walking where the Americans would run, and exhibiting a remarkable (in

American eyes) capacity to remain seated in one spot for long periods of time. A further illustration of this restraint is the ability of French children to play without getting their clothes dirty. A youngster will squat, poised over the sand or dirt in his elegant clothes, and only his hands become soiled. Periodically he shows his dirty hands to his mother; she cleans them, and he returns to play.

French children have a greater tolerance for solitary play than Americans. The adult who brings them to the park usually pays little further attention to them — except, of course, to prevent aggression, boisterous activity, or the exchange of property. Since the children quickly learn what behavior is not allowed, they spend most of their time alone, although others are playing nearby. They therefore learn to prefer playing alone, yet in the presence of others. This pattern conforms to the French tendency to consider the mere presence of others as a sort of sociability, even if no overt interaction occurs; it is a result of his childhood experience that the Frenchman finds it pleasant to sit alone with his drink and newspaper in a crowded café.

The way that French children play is an expression of the way their culture feels about children. Enjoyment of life is considered the prerogative of adults, and childhood is a necessary preparation for adulthood. Play must be useful and educational, never simply fun. The French see childhood as an unenviable state that has to be endured until one grows up. Americans hold an almost completely opposite view. We tend to regard childhood as an end in itself, an ideal age to be left reluctantly. Childhood is a time for freedom and play, and becoming an adult means exchanging this freedom for responsibility and work.

The difference between French and American children's play is only one example from a large body of sociological data that describe the function of play as a socializing factor, a means of transmitting the values and norms of a culture from one generation to another. Play is, in this sense, a tradition, a form of regulated and ritualized behavior that reproduces the regulations of the society in miniature. Children learn the rules of the adult world they will inhabit from the rules of their play as children. Both the best and the worst aspects of a society are first learned in play.

Once we become aware of the importance of play, we are faced with two alternatives. We may take the position that in play, as in life, what will be, will be, and we had best not tamper with the time-honored way of doing things. This position was succinctly expressed by a former Commissioner of Parks in New York City who reportedly stated, when asked his opinion of the standard playground that the Parks Department had been constructing for over thirty years, that what had been good enough for him was good enough for today's children.

The other alternative promises many more benefits both for our children and for the adult society they will inherit. It is to understand how play can either promote or discourage the values that we deem important, and to create an environment for play that will nurture the traits which reflect the highest aspirations of our society. We cannot create a condition of complete freedom for children, nor is this a desirable goal. Our traditions are a source of strength as well as weakness. What we can do is provide a fuller range of possibilities for play — we can design environments that are better suited to the needs of children and better suited, therefore, to the development of their full potential as healthy adults.

Rooftop Playground: New York City

In play, the behavior of the society is reproduced in miniature form.

the psychology of play 3

Youth is wholly experimental.

— Robert Louis Stevenson

The function of play in childhood has been essentially misunderstood in the past. Surprising numbers of people still maintain that the primary function of play is to "let off steam" so that the child can return to the more important business of study and learning. Countless studies of how intelligence develops in children show that precisely the reverse is true — that play is the way in which children develop intelligence. To put it simply, play is a child's way of learning.

Some understanding of the ways play and intelligence are related is essential if we wish to design play facilities that will encourage learning. Recent studies in developmental psychology combine the two formerly antagonistic main schools of thought about mental development: those who maintain that heredity is the determining factor, and those who hold that environment is more important.

In 1869, Francis Galton, the cousin of Charles Darwin, studied the biographical background of a thousand eminent men with a view to finding out if any unique qualities were present in their families. He found that men of great reputation in Great Britain tended to come from a

small group of families. From this, Galton concluded that genius is inherited, a conclusion heavily influenced by Darwin's conception of evolution as the survival of inherited characteristics. However, Galton neglected to consider the possibility that the children of these few privileged families not only had greater opportunity for experience and education, but also possessed family connections that made their efforts more successful than similar efforts by the children of less privileged groups.

At the other end of the heredity-environment spectrum are the behavioral psychologists, whose work is heavily influenced by Ivan Pavlov's studies of conditioning. Their attitude is exemplified by the claim made in 1924 by John B. Watson: "Give me a dozen healthy infants and my own specified world to bring them up in, and I'll guarantee to take any one of them and train them to become any type of specialist I might select — doctor, lawyer, artist, merchant chief, and yes, even beggarman and thief — regardless of his talents, penchants, tendencies, abilities, vocation and race of his ancestors." Thus, the behaviorists maintain that environment is the primary factor in the development of intelligence.

In fact, psychologists have been unable to credit either heredity or environment with a complete and exclusive role in the development of intelligence, and the evidence seems to indicate that both play a vital role in the growth of the individual. The interrelationship of the individual and his environment has been emphasized in many contemporary studies but perhaps is best expressed in the work of Jean Piaget. For more than thirty years, Piaget and his colleagues at the Rousseau Institute in Geneva, Switzerland, have been studying the development of intellectual functions in children. (It is interesting to note that in this age of technology and sophisticated laboratory equipment, Piaget first formulated his theories of the development of intelligence from the painstaking observation of his own three children during their early years.) The result of his work is a theoretical framework for understanding what intelligence is and how it develops, and a description of the stages of growth through which a child passes as he matures into an adult.

According to Piaget, intelligence is a special form of adaptation, which consists of a continuous creative interaction between the organ-

Play is a child's way of learning.

ism and the environment. Life thus becomes the process of creating increasingly complex structures of behavior. Neither the organism nor the environment exists alone, but only as they interact and affect each other. In computer parlance, this would be described as a situation with constant feedback of information: the organism acts, perceives its effect on the environment, and modifies its behavior to a more complex form to better cope with the environment.

Although the structures or frameworks through which we organize experience are constantly changing to reflect increasingly complex awareness of the world, the ways in which we create and modify these structures remain unchanged. Piaget conceives of two complementary processes — *assimilation* and *accommodation.*

Assimilation occurs when we see a new situation in terms of something familiar; when we act in a new situation as we have acted in past situations. Assimilation is the mastery of familiar or new skills by repetition and practice. Piaget defines it as "the action of the organism on surrounding objects, insofar as this action depends on previous behavior involving the same or similar objects." It is the inner organization of experience.

Accommodation is complementary to assimilation. It occurs when variations in the environment demand a modification in our pattern of behavior. Here the environment acts upon the organism, not by eliciting a fixed response based completely on previous experience, but by evoking a change of response to cope with the new situation. Accommodation occurs when a previously learned response fails to work in a new situation, and the organism modifies its response.

Assimilation and accommodation are the two processes by which the child gradually develops his intelligence from the primarily instinctual responses of infancy to the eventual achievement of adult logical thinking. This development takes place in stages, each of which has its characteristic forms of play.

*From birth to 18–24 months of age
(the sensorimotor phase)*

The infant is born with a group of reflexes that are instinctual (sucking, closing the hand around an object placed in it). From these passive responses he progresses rapidly to more active responses. The passive release of looking changes into the active search for objects. Reflexive crying changes into the active demand for food, expressing anger, or seeking relief from discomfort. The separate activities of the infant are coordinated during this period: he learns to follow the motion of his hand with his eyes and to control that motion. The infant learns that objects have permanence, and begins to look for things that have been removed from his field of vision. He begins to be aware of depth and space, and learns to maneuver in this space. He learns causality as he sees that his activity results in a corresponding change in his environment. He begins to observe the action of others and attempts to imitate their activity, as well as learning the separation of means and ends, thus being able to go through a series of simple steps to achieve a desired result. The end of the sensorimotor phase, with the learning of language, marks the emergence of genuine intelligence, but an intelligence still removed from the reflective intelligence of adults. In Piaget's words, "sensorimotor intelligence

Eiseman Nursery: New York City
Michael Altschuler, Designer

"Practice play" is characterized by repetition of an action
and delight in being the cause of an event. In the period
from birth to two years old, children learn to separate
means and ends and to go through a series of simple
steps to achieve a desired result.

Children translate their experience into a form that suits their inner needs. This is their way of understanding the things that happen to them.

acts like a slow-motion film, in which all the pictures are seen in succession but without fusion, and so without the continuous vision necessary for understanding the whole."

This phase is marked by what Piaget calls "practice play." The characteristics of practice play are repetition and pleasure in being the cause of an external event. An example of this play is the child who has recently discovered that when he lets go of an object it falls to the ground. Over and over he will pick it up and drop it again, each time exhibiting obvious delight. The constant repetition is a way of mastering the process of picking up and letting go for a child who is not completely sure that the dropped object will fall every time it is dropped. Whatever the project — dropping things, walking, filling a pail with sand — it is repeated with a great sense of urgency and intense concentration until the child feels that his performance is well within the range of his ability, at which time it will be replaced by another, more difficult, undertaking. The pleasure of being the cause of an event is an expression of the child's satisfaction with himself and his ability to control himself and his environment to some extent.

From 18–24 months to 4 years
(the preconceptual phase)

During this phase the child develops the ability to create symbols, to imitate the activities of others, and to learn language. Piaget shows that the creation of symbols — the representation of an external action or object by an internally created symbol — precedes the development of language in a child and is in fact a necessary prerequisite for that development. The development of symbolic thought means that the child can now differentiate between the symbol and the thing it symbolizes, a vast step toward the development of adult intelligence. At this point the child is no longer limited to the world of his immediate environment, for he can now create new situations in his imagination through the use of symbols.

"Symbolic play" is an essential part of the child's activity in these years. As practice play gave him a means for assimilating newly learned body skills, so does symbolic play furnish him with a way to assimilate the newly emerging skills of representing (symbolizing) objects and events. We are familiar with sym-

bolic play under the name "make-believe," or pretending. Children play at identifying one thing with another. Thus, a stick might become a boat or an airplane to a little boy, and he will make the stick go through the appropriate motions of the boat or plane; a little girl at the beach might play at serving an elaborate dinner on seashells. Another prevalent form of make-believe is imitation, in which the child plays at being another person. He might "be" a parent or an imaginary friend, and he will carry on long conversations with this new identity.

The content of symbolic play derives from the child's experience, which he shapes to suit his innermost needs. This is his way of understanding the things that happen to him — by reliving them in a simpler, safer, and more desirable form. Thus, a child who has had an unpleasant encounter with the family doctor might play at being a doctor, or both doctor and patient, in a situation somewhat removed from the pain of the actual experience and under his control. A child who has been forbidden some toy might play at receiving it to compensate for the deprivation. Symbolic play performs for the child the function that day-

dreaming performs for most adults — the opportunity to imagine ourselves in a gratifying situation where all our needs are met or where an unpleasant reality is altered. Symbolic play is a sort of wish fulfillment.

Until about the age of four, children are so involved with themselves that little attention is available for the activities of other children. They may play together, but their play is primarily individual. They do, however, enjoy the presence of other children in a condition of "parallel play," where each is immersed in a fantasy world of his own creation but occasional interaction takes place. This exposure to other children is important to prepare the way for the future, when a much greater degree of socializing occurs.

From 4 years to 7–8 years
(the intuitive phase)

This phase marks the child's growing ability to conceptualize — to organize his experience into increasingly logical concepts. True logic is not yet possible, and the child relies heavily on his intuition, but he is continually attempt-

ing to make his intuition correspond more closely to reality. This is the well-known stage of incessant questioning with which parents are so familiar. Questions help the child to correct his intuition and form the basis for future logical operations.

The social world of the child also begins to grow at this time, as he becomes aware of other children and strives to imitate their activities. This is a form of social behavior intermediate between purely individual and entirely social behavior. The child tries to understand (and thinks he does understand) the rules of the world of older children and adults, but he is actually very much isolated in his own point of view. Children now begin to play games with rules, but the rules are imperfectly understood and subject to widely different interpretations by each child.

This phase is one of transition — between the world of fantasy and the world of reality, between the world of intuition and the world of logical thinking, and between the world of solitary play and the world of social cooperation and mutual understanding.

Very young children may play together, but each is immersed in his own personal world. As they grow, they become aware of other children and begin to try to imitate their activities.

From 7–8 years to 11–12 years
(the concrete operations phase)

In these years, thought is progressively detached from perception or action, and the child becomes able to organize experience into the groupings of class, relation, and number. He begins to understand concepts such as the conservation of matter (the fact that a change in form, e.g., a lump of clay, does not result in an increased or decreased amount of matter) and reversibility (a series of steps can be done in reverse, bringing one to the point of original departure).

This phase is characterized by an intense interest in playing of games with rules, since the development of more systematic patterns of thought allows the child to enter into more complex social relationships. The ability to understand the reversibility of a process also makes it possible for one to appreciate the point of view taken by another individual. Most games with rules make their appearance when the child is about seven or eight years old, precisely because this marks the beginning of his ability to share with another person a com-

mon goal, and the capacity to recognize and to accept mutual responsibilities toward the achievement of that goal. This is the phase of social cooperation among children, when group activity and team efforts become possible and important.

At this time the child also becomes interested in the world of concrete objects and events. He wants to know how things work; he is curious about nature. The curiosity is "concrete" — it is best satisfied by the actual manipulation of the things in question and actual observation of the processes under study rather than abstract discussion about the principles involved. The child wants to see, smell, and touch for himself, and his curiosity can best be engaged and satisfied by firsthand experience.

From 11–12 years to 15–16 years
(the formal operations phase)

Adolescence marks the beginning of adult thought processes in the developing individual. Like an adult, the adolescent can deal with the *form* of an argument without necessarily being

When children become interested in the natural and man-made world, their curiosity is best satisfied by firsthand experience — actually doing, rather than abstract discussion.

concerned with its *content.* He can construct logical systems and no longer needs to confine his attention to existing reality. The process of detaching thought from perception or action, begun a few years before, is now complete, and the individual can now formulate theories and hypotheses that can be tested against reality. His is now an adult intelligence.

In terms of play, the adolescent's concern for the form of thoughts and events is manifested in a preoccupation with the rules of games. Not just concentrating on games with rules, as before, he becomes fascinated with anticipating all the possible situations that might arise in a game, and codifies rules to meet every contingency. The interest in regulations for their own sake expresses newly developed skills in creating logical systems, and the young person delights in creating situations that rival the complexity of adult situations.

Recognizing that people share common goals, and learning to work together toward these goals, is part of growing up.

criteria for design

4

The child's toys and the old man's reasons
are the fruits of the two seasons.

— William Blake

From a general discussion of the nature of play and its relationship to the learning process, we now come to the problem of establishing what is necessary for a successful play facility. One of the main difficulties confronting the designer is that play facilities are used by a number of distinct groups, each of which has requirements based on its own needs. The designer has to determine priorities among these often conflicting requirements. Once it is clear which are most critical, it becomes possible to resolve many of the secondary requirements as well. In fact, an understanding of the conflicting requirements can go a long way toward removing those very conflicts.

Following is a list of the main "users" of play facilities, in order of their degree of involvement.

Children

These little clients are, obviously, the most intimately affected by every aspect of the design — it is their interest, excitement, and curiosity that must be sustained and their personal safety that must be considered. But although they are the most deeply affected

Adventure Playground: London (Camden)

This facility was designed to fill the needs of those who are most directly affected by it — the children.

group of users, they are presently the least able to influence the design of their environment. Not only are children seldom consulted about these matters, but their needs are often completely forgotten when the facilities are being designed. The important decisions are made by another group at the other end of our spectrum of users. It is as if children were supplied with shoes with absolute disregard for the size of their feet — the size of the shoes having been determined by persons who would never have to wear them on the basis of what sizes were available.

Parents

After the children, this group has the greatest interest in the design of a successful play facility. Mature parents are very much concerned and will often go to great lengths to provide a good environment. The problem is the parent who is really satisfying personal needs in the name of providing for his children. (Recently, in a suburban home near New York, I asked my hosts how they decided to live in that location. The husband and wife both sighed and told me how much they missed their apartment in the city, and explained that they

decided to move to the country for the good of their children. The two teen-age sons for whom this sacrifice had been made fifteen years previously were stunned. They had both very much disliked growing up in their suburban community, traveled into the city at every opportunity, and had always believed that their parents preferred the suburbs. The parents were deeply surprised that the children shared their feelings about city life.)

Thoughtful parents, however, take great interest in trying to discover what the child's needs are, in distinction to their own. For example, a child's need for an environment where he can indulge his love of sand, water, and the resulting muddy mixture conflicts with his mother's desire to keep his clothes clean and his mouth free of tasty mud. A wise mother can set realistic priorities and relax her own demands somewhat for the sake of her child.

Parents can have an important influence on the design of play facilities, as a later chapter shows, but their role at present is usually limited. They are seldom consulted when play facilities are being planned, a situation that often results not only in obvious design mistakes that any mother could spot in an instant, but also in a feeling of hostility in the community toward the new play facility and those responsible for its construction.

Other Adults

This group is composed of all the adults who live or work in the vicinity of a play facility but are not parents of children who are currently using it. They too are affected by the design, as neighbors, spectators, and community members. Among them are elderly persons who enjoy watching children play, and local residents who resent having their morning sleep interrupted.

Although less immediately affected than parents, this group may actually have more influence on the final design of a playground. They generally are older than the parents; they have deeper roots in the community, and therefore exercise a greater degree of political control.

City Administration

This group comprises those who must supply and maintain the services and amenities of urban life, among which are playgrounds. They decide where, when, and what kind will be built, and they are faced with the problem of providing adequate facilities for play, from a usually inadequate budget, in competition with a host of other equally essential items.

This group of "users" exerts the greatest influence of all, yet it is also the group least affected by the results. City officials are usually too preoccupied with problems of finance and with political pressures from their constituents to consider whether the facilities they build are really suitable for children. And this is not because they are evil, impersonal bureaucrats, but simply because their energies are absorbed completely by the difficult demands placed upon them.

The spectrum of users, thus, ranges from the children who are totally affected by a facility about which they can have no say to the officials who wield total power over a problem of, at best, peripheral interest to them. Evidence that this system is at fault is all around us. In New York City alone, some three hundred playgrounds have been built according to these inverted values. It is useful to take a good look at a few of the results, since they illustrate almost the exact opposite of every quality desirable in a playground.

The typical New York playground (which is typical of 99 percent of all the playgrounds in the United States) could not be a more hostile environment for children's play if it had been designed for the express purpose of preventing play. Characteristically, it is an unbroken expanse of concrete or asphalt pavement, punctuated by the forlorn presence of metal swings, a slide, and some seesaws. Not only does this design lack any possibility for real play; the most interesting activities are prohibited anyway by signs saying "NO" in huge letters, followed by a list of all the things children like to do. The most admirable feature of these playgrounds is that they have been built to withstand the abuses of children and the ravages of time, and so may provide future historians with a wealth of archaeological material concerning that age in the development of our cities when ease of maintenance was an idea worshiped with near-religious fervor. A recent article in the *New York Times* summed up this attitude perfectly: "Several years ago two 350-pound gorillas were turned loose on a new set

Fort Hamilton Playground: New York City

For lack of other structures to engage their interest and attention, children crowd this modernized version of the iron jungle gym. Rubber matting has been added around it for safety, but the rest of the playground is mostly barren asphalt.

The typical American playground is an unbroken expanse of concrete or asphalt enlivened only by isolated swings, seesaws, and similar equipment.

Any playground is a learning experience. This little girl has invented a novel use for an ordinary piece of equipment — but if older children should come to play on the seesaws, she might easily get hurt.

of swings in Central Park. When it was found that the animals did not destroy the equipment, the playground was pronounced fit for New York City's children . . . The simplest maintenance measure, to be sure, would have been to exclude children, but that was clearly a Utopian solution."

This kind of playground conforms to the requirements of administrators — it is simple to build, indestructible, and noncontroversial. It is another story when the children's requirements are considered. The concrete or asphalt paving is brutal to heads and elbows and knees. The indestructible steel swings are just the right height to menace the destructible children playing near them. The slides furnish a drop of over seven feet to the pavement, and their ladders are so narrow that a child does not have the option of changing his mind once he begins the upward climb. A child whose attention wavers momentarily can be seriously injured by a fall from the seesaw; the tiny sandboxes create dangerous congestion among the toddler population, and so on. The list of possible injuries is long and varied, and has resulted in the strange spectacle of mothers organizing to demand the *removal* of equipment from their playground.

Another fault of the typical playground is its total lack of anything to inspire interest or curiosity. After a little swinging and sliding and seesawing, the built-in opportunities for play are exhausted. Children, however, are not so simpleminded as adults, and the name of a piece of equipment does not deter them from inventing uses for it beyond the designers' and administrators' wildest imaginings. Swings become hanging battering rams for an exciting and noisy battle; children with nerves of steel play swing-the-swing-around-the-top-in-a-full-circle. Seesaws make excellent catapults and are great for the jump-off-while-your-partner-is-up-in-the-air game. And after these limited and perilous options are used up, there are the games of destruction, in which children pit their ingenuity — and anger — against the designers of these play facilities for 350-pound gorillas. The final expression of the frustration of the otherwise powerless children is the scrawling of obscene remarks on the unyielding and inhospitable asphalt. The children know that whoever created this place did not

care about them, and they learn not to care about it and those who built it.

Even a poorly designed playground is a learning experience for children, and what they learn becomes a part of the way they see the world around them and the persons who inhabit this world. The lessons they learn in the "gorilla" playgrounds are profoundly disturbing, and can be seen at work in the adult world. They learn, first, that they do not matter as individuals but only as a group whose needs for play facilities must be met even though in the most minimal way. They learn that they can have no constructive effect on their fixed and immobile environment; they can change it only in a destructive way, finding satisfaction by outwitting the adult world so evidently hostile to them. They learn that the man-made world is dull, ugly, and dangerous, and empty of sensuous satisfactions; that civilization delights in reducing the varied potentials and unique qualities of individuals to a pattern of uniformity; that pleasure can be obtained only at the expense of another individual — a solitary pleasure, incapable of being shared with others.

Thus, the children grow into adults obsessed with the accumulation of things, unable to communicate with others, and insensitive to the world around them. They become parents and they teach their children, as they were taught, that life is work, that work is dull, and that dullness is all that can ever be expected from a life on which they can have little effect.

To blame all these things solely on the design of playgrounds is as naive as thinking that well-designed play facilities are all that is needed to produce healthy children who will grow into healthy adults — both these ideas are obviously untrue. The truth is that every aspect of our world affects us in some way, even if we cannot say precisely how, and this is especially true for children. The entire fabric of our environment is important, and therefore an improvement made in any portion of it is important.

Now that we have seen the full range of groups whose needs must for one reason or another be taken into account by the designer, let us consider the genuine requirements of each.

The most interesting place in a typical playground is the drinking fountain, the site of an endless stream of activity — and water. Swings and slides may lie idle after a while, but there are unlimited possibilities for play with water.

Drawing by Robert Kraus. Copyright 1967, The New Yorker Magazine, Inc.

City Administrations

Cost

The single most important drawback to the construction of well-designed playgrounds, administrators will tell you, is their cost. Although it is true that playgrounds which really allow for play are slightly more expensive than the usual asphalt desert, comparing absolute costs is misleading and inaccurate. If the asphalt desert costs $50,000 to build and is *used* by 5,000 children in a typical year, it is not cheaper than the creative playground that might cost $100,000 to build and is used by 50,000 children — it actually costs five times as much. The only measure that can reflect how well the money has been spent is use, the *cost per use.* This measure is in the language that administrators understand and respond to, and as such is useful in rebutting their often misguided attempts at thriftiness. Much more important than this quantitative measure is the qualitative one — what is the experience of the children who use the facility. But, unfortunately, many persons, probably products of the asphalt-desert school of playground design, only respond to things that can be counted or

"It's not your sandbox. It's the city's sandbox."

otherwise classified, and the cost-per-use yardstick speaks to them.

Maintenance

The illusion of the "maintenance-free" playground should be dispelled from the minds of all those responsible for the construction of play facilities. Architects are particularly to blame for the spread of this unfortunate myth, which has done much to foster suspicion of good design and innovation among those whom we charge to maintain the facilities. Some playgrounds do require less maintenance than others, but any place where real play occurs must be cared for, kept free of dangerous materials, cleaned, and replenished when necessary. But though a well-designed playground must be maintained, costs due to vandalism and destructive play usually will be greatly reduced, and this to some extent balances the increased maintenance cost.

Proper maintenance also serves to extend the useful life of a facility, and thus to distribute its cost over a long period of time. A deteriorating playground simply encourages children to add to the general destruction, while a well-kept place actually enlists the support and efforts of children to keep it that way.

Education

Since play is actually a child's way of learning about his environment and about himself, administrators ought to stop thinking of playgrounds as athletic facilities. The playground is as important a learning institution as a school, and should be given equivalent priority. The vision of a public school classroom devoid of books, teachers, blackboards, and furniture would give a city administrator apoplexy, but a similar situation in a playground passes for normal in all but the most forward-looking American communities.

Other Adults

A playground can be a source of satisfaction to many adults beside the parents of the children playing in them. (It might in fact, be easier for a disinterested adult to enjoy the goings-on of the children because he is not so intimately involved.) The play of children is endlessly fascinating, and it brings to many of us memories of our own childhood. Old persons, particularly, enjoy watching children play, and this should be taken into account in selecting the location of a new play facility. A playground is like a little theater in which most of the "players" are delightfully oblivious of their audience. The spectator-sport aspect of play facilities should not be overlooked.

The joy of watching children at play can be matched in intensity only by the discomfort of being blasted from peaceful sleep by the cacophony of exuberant children. An aspect of playground design that is often overlooked is the location of such a facility too near to bedroom windows.

Parents

Safety

It is obvious that from the parents' point of view a good playground is one that meets their children's needs by providing the greatest possible latitude for meaningful play. But this criterion is qualified by one major condition. The factor of safety is actually more important to parents than any other. It has been the cause of their dissatisfaction with present facilities and has led them to encourage innovation in design. A safe playground frees parents from constant anxious attention to their children's activities and allows them to relax and enjoy *their* time in the playground. The realization that adults spend as much time in playgrounds as children may come as a surprise to many of us, but it has important implications for playground design.

Separation from Adults

Parents should be able to put some slight distance between themselves and their children for purposes of quiet or socializing with other adults. There is one important provision, however. While, if the playground is safe it is not necessary that parents always be able to see their children at play, it is very important that the children be able to see their parents. The reasons for this are considered below, from the children's point of view.

Comfort

Since adults spend hours in playgrounds, it is essential that thought be given to the facilities provided for them. Such details are important

Children's Zoo: Rapperswil (Zurich)

The most important criterion for a playground, from the parent's point of view, is that it be safe for children to play in. But adequate seating facilities from which parents can watch without being in the midst of the activity, and protection from the sun, can make trips to the playground enjoyable for adults as well as children.

because they make the difference between a playground that is used and enjoyed by parents and one that is at best endured, but often avoided. Benches should be comfortable and arranged to accommodate both those who wish to sit alone and those who choose to congregate. There must be space for strollers and baby carriages, since many mothers bring two or more children at a time. Adequate shade is very important, or even a well-designed playground will be deserted on hot days. Toilet facilities for children and adults should be located nearby. (It should be noted, however, that toilet facilities are expensive to build, and must be supervised constantly to keep them clean and free of loiterers.)

Accessibility

Although parents will go to considerable trouble and travel some distance to take their children someplace different from the usual playground, it should not be necessary to go far afield to find a good playground that is not overcrowded. Ideally, there should be different types of playgrounds, including small sidewalk play areas in each block and a more elaborate, supervised playground serving a whole neighborhood.

Children

The list of criteria that follows has its origin in the premise that intelligence and learning consist of a creative interaction between the individual and his environment. This statement contains the two primary reqirements for the design of play environments, and from these all the other requirements are derived. The first is that the environment must provide the individual with an adequate range of experience. The second is that the environment must allow for some measure of control by the individual. (As the next chapter shows, these are precisely the conditions sought by children when they are left to their own devices.) The British psychiatrist Ronald Laing has called these two interrelated factors "experience" and "control of experience," and states that they are essential for any individual to live a healthy human life.

The absence of either of these factors creates a dehumanized environment in which it is almost impossible to develop as a person. The total lack of sensory stimuli can result in permanent brain damage and even death, as in the disease called infantile marasmus, which was at one time common in institutions where

If the junk in this vacant lot were clean and free of rats, the site would be a more suitable playground than the asphalt desert in which these children might be playing — but are not. The filthy and dangerous lot provides what its municipal alternative usually does not: variety of experience and an opportunity to interact with the environment.

infants were adequately fed but deprived of any additional human contact. The devastating effect of an environment that deprives the individual of sensory experience is seen in the soldiers who were brainwashed during the Korean War: they were prepared to accept the distorted reality of their captors by solitary confinement and the elimination of any familiar experience. In the German concentration camps of World War II, the prison situation operated to rob the individual of his sense of humanity by eliminating his control over his world. It has been shown that most of those who survived that experience were persons who managed to keep some aspect of their daily life under their personal control.

One of the most disturbing aspects of our modern technological society is that it is full of experience and sensory stimuli, but increasingly less under the control of most individuals. The recent riots in the slums of our cities are an expression of ghetto-dwellers' frustration resulting from their inability to have an effect on their environment. The need to make some mark on the world one lives in is as fundamental as the need for food and shelter, but it is much more difficult to satisfy.

Adventure Playground: London (Paddington)

This playground is filled with a selection of junk that is safe as well as fun to play with. Under the watchful (but unobtrusive) eye of a supervisor, children can rearrange their physical world to their liking — one way to exert some control over their experience.

Experience

A playground should be like a small-scale replica of the world, with as many as possible of the sensory experiences to be found in the world included in it. Experiences for every sense are needed, for instance: rough and smooth objects to look at and feel; light and heavy things to pick up; water and wet materials as well as dry things; cool materials and materials warmed by the sun; soft and hard surfaces; things that make sounds (running water) or that can be struck, plucked, plinked, etc.; smells of all varieties (flowers, bark, mud); shiny, bright objects and dull, dark ones; things both huge and tiny; high and low places to look at and from; materials of every type, natural, synthetic, thin, thick, and so on. The list is inexhaustible, and the larger the number of items on it that are included, the richer and more varied the environment will be for the child.

Control of Experience

Once we have provided a place overflowing with things to see, touch, smell, hear, and taste, we must encourage the interaction of the child

Adventure Playground: London (Cable Street)

The inside of a piano, lumber, cardboard, and an old automobile seat were combined to make a weatherproof clubhouse that is child-sized and private.

with them. The materials must be able to "respond": things that can be burrowed in, piled in heaps, thrown, carried, sifted, eaten, pounded, pushed, slapped, dammed, collected in vessels, spilled, floated on, drunk, and splashed. If, because of some strange circumstances, a playground had to be limited to only two materials, water and sand would provide more possibilities for play and fun than all the "asphalt deserts" combined. If sand is not available, ordinary dirt is a satisfactory substitute — although perhaps not from a mother's point of view.

Another way to exert control over one's world is to rearrange the things in it. In addition to paper, paint, and glue, almost any cast-off material is satisfactory for this process of assemblage (and dis-assemblage), including old tires, scrap lumber (with edges rounded), rope, cable spools, bamboo poles, canvas and burlap sacks, blocks, automobile parts, old mattresses, chairs, cardboard cartons — again the list is endless. It is limited only by the availability of materials and the requirements of safety — obviously razor blades and gunpowder should be kept from children. (A close friend once related to me how he and his

friends, then ten or eleven years old, had spent the war years in Warsaw accumulating gunpowder from unexploded shells to make firecrackers — a frightening kind of creative interaction between children and their environment.)

The simple action of moving things in one's environment is another way to control it. Swings and seesaws are movable, but their motion is predictable and fixed within rigid bounds. More interesting are things with movement that is unpredictable or related more closely to the actions of the person in or on it. Professor Joseph Brown of Princeton University has designed several pieces of equipment that not only move in response to the movement of each child, but also affect every other person on them. This motion is at once complex and personal, and teaches the children the valuable lesson that they are all together on the structure and that their every action affects every other person — a lesson many of us have yet to learn.

The ability to move over, under, around, or through something also affords a child control: he can change his relationship to it (and there-

Adventure Playground: London (Camden)

A playground should present a variety of challenges ranging from things young children can master to things that require the skill and agility of older children. The structures in this playground can be used in many ways and at many levels. The cargo net is one route for scaling the low tower; ropes and timbers provide other approaches. The discarded cable spools can be used for climbing and rolling or as tables.

To move over, under, around, or through things is to affect the environment by changing one's relationship to it. Within the small world of this playground the children have made a combination slide, swing, and jungle gym (or fort, ship, or mountain) very different from the standard playground equipment.

fore its relation to him). The point is to provide as many different ways of relating as possible.

Graduated Challenge

Learning, we have seen, is a combination of repeating the performance of something we already know in order to perfect it (assimilation) and mastering new things requiring new combinations of skills and ability (accommodation). An environment that provides only the familiar, challenges that already have been overcome countless times, will never call forth any new learning. Similarly, a place that is too challenging creates too large a gap between what children feel confident of through past experience and the new task, thereby overwhelming rather than encouraging them.

A playground therefore should present a series of challenges, ranging from simple things that toddlers can master to ones that challenge older and more experienced children. There should be continuity, so that each child always has the dual experience of having mastered some aspects of his environment while knowing there are other aspects that he may still aspire to master. As in adult life, the individual

Although realistic forms can be obstacles to the free play of imagination, these giant objects (below and opposite page) are not. Enormous in scale, they are first of all mountains to climb and only secondarily human forms — and fantastic ones at that.

who feels he has accomplished everything and the one who is so overwhelmed that he is unable to accomplish anything have both reached a point where further growth and development are impossible.

Another advantage of play facilities incorporating a broad spectrum of activities is that children of different ages may coexist peacefully, learning from and teaching each other but sufficiently separated by their skills and abilities to keep the young children safely out of the way of the older ones.

Choice

Choice is quite an important way of controlling one's environment. A playground may provide children with various kinds of choice. A child should be able to decide whether to play alone, with a small group of children, or with a large group. Each of these options implies a distinct kind of space: small, sheltered areas for solitary play, more ample places for small groups, and an open space for group activity. The moods of a child are mercurial, and he should have an environment that is receptive whether he feels active or passive. We must

remember that his mind is active and exploring even when his body is at rest. (In general, Americans are suspicious of physical inactivity. Loitering, for which one can be arrested in the United States, is the national pastime of France, Italy, and Spain. The Puritan warning, "A rolling stone gathers no moss," needs very much the Biblical antidote, "Consider the lilies of the field, they toil not, neither do they spin.")

The child should also be able to choose when he will undertake a risky (to him) activity. For example, as noted before, slides are presently designed so a child cannot change his mind once he has begun to climb the ladder because he is immediately blocked from behind by a line of fearless sliders who clamor for him to hurry up, and often give their obstacle (by now terrified) a push to clear the path. Any piece of equipment should give children the chance to perform a reconnaissance, to go part way, while preserving the possibility of retreat until a more propitious moment.

Exercise of Fantasy

Since one of the ways that a child learns about the world is by "playing" at different roles in his imagination, it is very important to allow for choice in this activity. Lately there has been great interest in playground equipment built in the shape of fire engines, horses, submarines, rocket ships, and other such objects from the real world. Although these are of momentary interest to children, they seem designed primarily to satisfy adults, who need to have a name or label for things before they feel at ease. Children can create their imaginary world from simpler — and cheaper — things: mounds of dirt, empty boxes, the branch of a tree. In fact, the more general a form or object is, the more freedom it seems to allow the children to impose their own meaning on it. Thus, a cardboard box can be a boat, car, house, rocket ship, submarine, horse, swimming pool, or almost anything else. The fabricated submarine or horse, on the other hand, is too insistent in its meaning and leaves little latitude for the exercise of fantasy.

Separation from Adults

The need for some means of separating parents from their children has already been mentioned. This is a controversial subject, so it is important to define carefully what is meant by

**Children's Creative Center, Expo 67: Montreal
Cornelia Hahn Oberlander, Landscape Architect**

A good supervisor will lend a helping hand if asked, but can keep an eye on everything without interfering.

**Adventure Playground, Central Park: New York City
Richard Dattner, Architect**

A supervisor can give assistance without the emotional involvement of a parent.

separation. Obviously, a parent must be able to reach his child quickly if the child is in danger or some serious difficulty. It is also important for a child to have the security of knowing that his parent is nearby, to be able to see his parent when he needs reassurance or simply wishes to demonstrate some newly found skill. Separation is desirable, however, when a parent does not feel the child is in trouble but would be tempted to interfere if the child were too near. Children need the freedom to make mistakes, to be clumsy and fall, without an ever-present parent who, with a misguided desire to help the child avoid all disappointment and pain, interferes with the natural process of trial and error by which we all learn. A supervisor often combines the good features of a parent — providing a model and helping children over difficult moments when they undertake more than they can handle — while avoiding excessive concern that is difficult for the parent to control. One of the most interesting games that children play consists of hiding behind something and shouting to their parents, "I see you but you can't see me!" This phrase sums up an essential aspect of being a child — delight in the freedom and power to act independently while keeping security, in the form of a parent, safely in sight.

Expressive Play

For a trained person, a well-designed playground can be an efficient tool for helping children with special problems. Play can be used both to diagnose a child's difficulties and to help him with them. We can hardly expect most playgrounds to have either the facilities or the expert staff necessary to evaluate how a child's play reflects his unconscious feelings, but these are very important considerations in designing playgrounds for children with exceptional problems, whether emotional, physical, or mental (or, as is usually the case, a combination of all of these).

The criteria discussed in this chapter cannot all be met in every playground, but they do represent a goal to aim for and a yardstick by which existing and proposed facilities may be evaluated. They are based on the premises that play is learning, that a properly designed environment is conducive to meaningful play, and that city administrators, parents, and our society as a whole all have a stake in the outcome. All the requirements listed here are important, but two are indispensable: children must play in an environment which provides them with experience, and they must have the opportunity to control that experience.

children as designers

5

*The games of children . . . are their most
serious business.*

— Michel de Montaigne

Just as Piaget's theories about the development of children were derived from a careful observation of children, the designer of playgrounds must base his ideas on the experience of watching how children play when left alone. A phenomenon that can be seen in almost any city is a group of children playing in the street, while a nearby playground is deserted. Using the raw materials of the street, these children create a lively environment far richer and more interesting than the playground, even though it is also far more dangerous.

Although children probably have always played with building materials and junk, the first recorded attempt to utilize this instinct in the design of a playground occurred in Denmark in 1943. Professor C. T. Sorensen, a well-known landscape architect, had noticed that children preferred to play in junkyards and building sites rather than in the playgrounds set up for their use. In a new housing development outside of Copenhagen he started the Emdrup Playground, which was furnished with waste materials and had a full-time supervisor.

The contrast between the way that children

and adults react to such playgrounds is striking. Children are immediately at ease amidst the "junk." Finding some order and harmony in piles of building materials and debris, they quickly set to work rearranging them to suit some elaborate and highly personal plan. Adults, on the other hand, seldom see anything more than confusion, chaos, and danger, despite assurances by experienced supervisors that these playgrounds are generally much safer than the ordinary ones because the children are constantly busy and alert and seldom need to resort to destructive types of play, a frequent cause of serious accidents. The message is as clear as the children know how to make it — they want to create their own kind of order based on criteria quite different from those of adults. They want to design their own playgrounds. A few examples may illustrate the basis of the children's choice and indicate what a playground needs to make it come alive for them.

A rope tied to the top of a fire escape on a deserted building makes a spectacular — and dangerous — swing.

This little girl actually broke her leg playing on these wires but could not resist returning to the challenging environment of the vacant lot.

What some people discard is treasure to others.

These boys take turns directing a powerful stream of water with a tin can. Passing cars and other children are the favorite targets.

Water

A fire hydrant on New York's Lower East Side has been turned on during a hot summer morning, and a number of overlapping play activities are going on around it. The first is a game requiring quite a bit of strength from the little boys who are engaged in it. They stand in an orderly line on the dry side of the hydrant, waiting to take their turn on the firing line. The boy at the head of the line is channeling the water stream through a small can from which both ends have been cut. He can hit with great accuracy anything that moves within twenty-five yards. After a few seconds, the next boy in line moves to the front and the previous marksman takes his place at the rear of the line. Cars are the favorite targets, and the children have an uncanny ability to spot drivers who disapprove of their activity, giving them a full broadside shot. With a tremendous amount of water pressure at their command (it normally takes two firemen to handle a fire hose), the kids are suddenly a match for all the adults who have previously harassed them, and the soaking confrontation provides them with some measure of justice. Many drivers stop to inveigh against the children (from behind closed

windows), but none is foolish enough to leave his sanctuary, and all eventually drive away. The few drivers who in a decent manner actually ask the children to lower the spray so they can pass are often rewarded by equally decent behavior on the part of the youngsters.

Across the street, at the other end of the water stream, an entirely different game is in progress between cars. Here the object is to avoid the spray, primarily as a test of speed and skill against the accuracy of the amateur firemen, and not at all to stay dry. (Few children want to be dry on a hot day, and those who do are careful to stay well down the block.) The spray is lowered and the kids edge closer within firing range, while the marksmen across the street exhibit a remarkable nonchalance. Suddenly a tin can is clamped over the stream, a great squeal goes up from the intended victims as they retreat, and shouts of victory or disappointment, depending on the outcome, rise from the dripping, smiling firemen. The cycle is repeated, with minor variations in cast and plot, all day long and into the night.

Meanwhile, the water has accumulated in the

gutters and is flowing toward the drain at the corner. Farther down the block a little boy has dammed the stream with some cobblestones (taken from the street), creating a lagoon; half-a-dozen children are wading in it or sunning themselves along the edge. Two girls on the sidewalk are following toy boats floating on the end of strings in the rapids just before the drain. A little boy squats over the drain and looks into the murky depths below, perhaps imagining subterranean encounters between sewer repairmen and giant alligators grown from Florida souvenirs flushed down toilets long ago. All this joy is usually quite illegal (and sometimes dangerous, because it reduces water pressure in the hydrants), and often a policeman comes to turn off the water. Sprinklers are available to decrease the water loss, but they are not the same — the spray can't be aimed and doesn't produce enough water to suitably flood the street.

It isn't the beach, but it is close to home.

Nothing is wasted. The water from the hydrant is dammed with cobblestones, creating a small lake and a waterfall. Farther down the block, water is collected in handy containers for use in other projects.

Beer cans are round and shiny and make a fine clatter when kicked into the street. Many discarded products of our industrial society make excellent play materials.

Junk

A little boy is standing in a filthy street, which apparently is not on the maps of the Department of Sanitation. He carefully selects an armful of shiny, empty beer cans and proceeds to line them up on the sidewalk. He works with great patience, getting the cans to line up exactly, until everything is the way he wants it. Then he stands behind the cans and kicks them noisily, one by one, into the street. When they are all in the street, he begins again with as much care as before.

Across the street, another boy is pushing a discarded milk carton around and around, like a driver on a miniature racecourse. He is completely absorbed. It is not possible for an adult watching him ever to know what the milk carton has become in his imagination.

The same little boy who was kicking the cans now takes them across the street to the steps of a church. There he finds a box that once contained soft-drink bottles, and he turns it on its side. Starting from one corner, he puts a beer can in every slot, from left to right in each row, until all the slots are filled.

Cartons and crates come in an endless variety of sizes. They can be stacked, pushed, and sat in, and they are probably the most sought-after junk for play.

In some playgrounds, a pile of leaves and dirt is the most interesting thing around.

Dirt

Using their hands and an assortment of toy earth-moving equipment, two boys are digging a pit in a patch of dirt. After reaching an appropriate depth (following a great deal of discussion about what depth is the proper depth), they balance a discarded pipe in the hole and remove all the toy equipment to a safe distance. The hole is a rocket-launching site, and a countdown begins.

An infant barely old enough to walk half pauses, half falls in a pile of dirt and dead leaves in a barren playground. He touches the mixture with his hand and discovers that it is both interesting to feel and difficult to pick up. He patiently practices picking up a handful and dropping it; after a while he is covered with dirt and leaves, but this only adds to the fun, and he continues until he has mastered the art. Now he discovers that the leaves also taste good — but at this point his mother plucks him from the dirt pile and reinstalls him on the asphalt in front of her bench.

In many playgrounds, a lot of activity centers around the base of the trees, while nearby play

This ingenious boy has found that a huge flattened-out carton makes a soft and slippery slide.

Adventure Playground: London (St. John's Wood)

This playground may look dangerous, but it is not — the structures in it were built to be used by children, and supervision is provided.

equipment is ignored. The attraction is the dirt, which can be dug into, scraped, compacted, or mixed with water from the water fountain.

Watching children playing in city streets brings us back to our starting point — our observation of the interaction of children with their environment. Faced with a choice between the places designed for them by adults and the far more stimulating and dangerous street environment, the children choose the latter. When confined to a barren playground, they choose to play with dirt around trees or the drinking fountains, while largely passing by the play equipment. Left alone, they choose an environment rich in experience — experience over which they have some measure of individual control. Children given the opportunity and the raw materials will design a playground far better than most facilities designed for them by adults.

Many European playgrounds do precisely that: like the Emdrup Playground mentioned at the beginning of this chapter, they furnish a site, building materials, water, a leader to watch over things and offer help when it is needed, and nothing more. The children are left free to

Telephone cables are ideal for high-wire acrobatics, but a fall in a vacant lot full of debris could cause serious injuries.

Adventure Playground: London (Camden)

This rigging can be used for acrobatics too, but there is little chance of falling from it — and if a child should fall, the ground below is cleared of broken glass and rusty nails. In addition, the cargo net is supported in several places, so if one rope breaks, others will hold it up.

make of all this material whatever they like; once they have built something they may change it or tear it down. The level of organization maintained by the leader varies with the age of the children who use the playground. Materials and tools that are simple to handle are provided for the very young, and the leader keeps a careful eye on them to see that their structures are strong enough to support their weight. It is recognized that older children are able to maintain interest in a project over a fairly long period, and a wider range of tools and materials is supplied for them.

There are also playgrounds designed for ten- to fifteen-year-olds that are divided into small building plots, the use of which is granted to one child for an entire summer. In the course of the summer, the young tenants build their own houses according to their own plans. Help is offered by the leader only when requested, and other children must be invited before they may enter someone else's lot. At the summer's end, the children take down their constructions and leave the site ready for the next year's builders. Children over the age of fifteen may participate only if the younger tenants ask their help. Teamwork is not discouraged, but it is

Adventure Playground: London (St. John's Wood)

Children helped to build this precarious-looking tower, which was checked for structural stability and pronounced safe by the playground supervisor.

left to the discretion of the participants and not imposed by the leader.

That this plan would be a success in the United States seems evident from the following anecdote, related to me by the general contractor of a large playground and community facility. Every morning, the job superintendent found an electrical generator disassembled, the parts neatly stacked next to each other, undamaged. The night watchman finally deduced that a group of children would nightly work for several hours to dismantle the machine (not an easy job by any means), pitting their skill against that of the workmen who daily had to reassemble it. The goal of the children was not necessarily malicious — the prank was simply an expression of their skill and ingenuity. In vain it was suggested that the superintendent leave the generator in parts one evening to see if it would be miraculously reassembled the next morning. Given the means, the children might have been even more enthusiastic over the possibility of constructing something to exercise their talent.

With the proper supervision, it should be possible simply to deliver a load of building materials to a previously cleared site and let the local kids make their own playground. Not only would the cost of such a place be but a fraction of the usual playground, but vandalism would be highly unlikely, with the proud builders zealously guarding their handiwork.

adventure playground - a case history

6

The next best thing to a playground designed entirely by children is a playground designed by an adult but incorporating the possibility for children to create their own places within it. This chapter is the case history of such a playground.

The Background

The history of the Adventure Playground on the west side of Central Park in New York City began some eight years before the actual construction commenced. An old playground (one of twenty virtually identical facilities built around the perimeter of the park just after the Depression) that stood on the site was to be demolished to provide a parking lot, and the City Department of Parks built a somewhat smaller playground nearby as a replacement for the one to be razed. Some local mothers noticed the arrival of the bulldozers, ran home to get reinforcements, and returned in force, with baby carriages, to block the path of the bulldozers. The project was dropped, the mothers went home, and things returned to normal again, except that now there were two playgrounds right next to each other.

All the illustrations in this chapter are of the Adventure Playground in Central Park, New York City. The playground was a gift of the Estée and Joseph Lauder Foundation to the City of New York, and was designed by the author.

About six years later, another generation of children and mothers was using the playgrounds. One day, after a child playing on a slide was badly hurt in a fall (one in a long history of injuries), three mothers having coffee together decided that something should be done to prevent future accidents. They felt that the equipment was dangerous and inadequate, and that improper maintenance made things even worse. They decided to petition the Parks Commissioner for rubber safety surfacing under the equipment, adequate maintenance, and some additional recreation facilities. They obtained over 800 signatures, as well as letters to the Parks Department from community organizations and leaders. They then met with the Commissioner, who agreed to provide better maintenance, predicted that some rubber surfacing might be available in about four years, and flatly refused to provide any additional recreation facilities. (It was this Commissioner who reportedly averred that since the existing playgrounds had been adequate for him when he was young, he could not understand any objections to their present value). The mothers concluded that it would be a waste of their time and effort to fight the

Parks Department, and they resolved to seek their own source of funds and use their own energy to change things. As a first step, they organized a Sunday event in the playground, where volunteer parents picked up *three bushels* of glass fragments from the ground.

Meanwhile, the administration of New York City changed hands, and with it the post of Parks Commissioner. The new Commissioner was a young man of great energy and enthusiasm, willing to try new ideas, and anxious to restore the parks to the people. With the support of the administration, he closed several city parks, including Central Park, to vehicular traffic on Saturdays (later this was extended to Sundays and two evenings a week). The parks began to fill with thousands of people, on foot and on bicycles (so popular were the bicycles that a thriving industry grew on sales and rentals). Sharing a general feeling of hope concerning the parks, a feeling that perhaps something coud be done, the West Side mothers again approached the Parks Department and this time found support. Financing was now needed. Donors for construction projects are usually not so hard to find as one might think — the many statues and memorials yearly given to every city (not to mention the generous number of inappropriate gifts that are refused) bear witness to their existence. But it is very difficult to find sponsors with the courage to underwrite an experimental project and the confidence to face a group of local residents. Miraculously, however, one appeared — a private foundation that had recently begun to investigate a number of sites around the city with a view to building an "adventure" playground on the model of several that had recently been opened in Europe.

The mothers' committee grew rapidly as word spread that a new playground really would be built. The foundation retained an architect (the author) at this early stage, so that he could help in the selection of the site and join in preliminary meetings with the community. It was time to begin designing the playground.

Planning

Some time before the Adventure Playground project developed, a wealthy donor had offered the city a large playground designed by a well-known architect and sculptor in collaboration.

The design was very imaginative and should have been a welcome addition to the city, but the local residents were angered because they had not been consulted, and felt that the project was being forced on them. There were many controversies, complex and overlapping, which not only kept the neighborhood in an uproar for years, but even alienated friends as people chose sides in the dispute. A major subject of contention was that the new playground would replace a pleasant, much-used landscaped area on a hill. The residents suggested moving the playground farther down the hill to a more suitable place, but the donor refused and the project died under the continuing protests of the community.

Although never built, this playground had a considerable influence on subsequent playgrounds, including the Adventure Playground. In addition to its outstanding design, the doomed project yielded one very important lesson: the community must be fully involved in a project from its inception. The first problem we faced, therefore, was how and at what point to involve the community in the actual designs for the Adventure Playground. To meet after it had been planned completely was out

of the question, for the reasons just discussed, but we felt that meeting with the local residents too soon—that is, before we had even formulated the basic concepts of the project — might be confusing and lead to hours spent discussing irrelevant subjects. We finally resolved to prepare some very sketchy designs illustrating what might be done in an "adventure" playground and to present them to the mothers' committee for their comments and suggestions.

The first meeting, with the directors and active members of the committee, was an informal one held at the home of one of the members in order to encourage free discussion. At the beginning, I made a verbal presentation to explain the background of this new type of play facility and to describe how it differed from playgrounds around the city. The mothers were far ahead of me in their dissatisfaction with existing facilities, since they daily faced the dual problems of keeping their children busy and safe. Not surprisingly, they were enthusiastic about the prospect of any departure from what they too well knew was inadequate.

In the sketches, which were now shown, some

A crude scale model of the proposed design formed the basis for discussions with the community. Suggested modifications included the elimination of the central pool and water channel from this area; additional tunnels into the volcano (upper right); entrances for small children in the crater (foreground); and a low tower and a flagpole at the main entrance (partially seen at left).

of the general concepts that had been discussed were applied to the specific conditions and limitations of the site. The drawings gave a good idea of what the new facility might look like, without being too detailed or definite about any aspect of the design. As a result, the mothers could relate the ideas to personal experience with their children and were able to suggest many modifications based on their knowledge. Had the meeting been held simply to ask each person what she wanted, it would have produced a list of highly individual demands, followed by great disappointment when many suggestions were omitted, for whatever reason, from the plans. The format of this meeting, however, provided an opportunity to utilize each individual's experience and knowledge to modify general concepts endorsed by everyone.

A subsequent meeting with the entire group of mothers was scheduled, and it was agreed that a rough scale model of the design would be presented at that time. In the meantime, the participants in the initial meeting had an opportunity to talk to the other members, so that everyone would be at least partially familiar with the plans.

The second meeting was a more formal one held in a community meeting room and attended by about seventy persons. After a brief recapitulation of my introductory statement at the first meeting, slides were projected, showing the original drawings and the newly prepared scale model. The audience was not only larger than the first, but also more diverse, including quite a few husbands interested for the first time. This diversity was reflected in the much wider range of questions asked after the presentation. New questions were raised and there was some heated debate. A typical argument concerned toilet facilities. Several parents wanted to include in the new design this convenience which was too costly to build without eliminating important educational features. It was finally decided that the existing nearby facilities would continue to be used, and the Parks Department would be asked to provide new toilets. (They were asked, but did not have adequate funds.)

The meeting also had its lighter moments. One mother complained that a stray horse had recently entered the playground and frightened the children. What, she asked, would the new design do about *that*? I suggested that the standard signs which prohibit almost every form of activity in city playgrounds be amended to include "NO HORSES."

Near the end of the meeting, the donors made a special request. They had agreed to pay for the construction of the playground and the architect's fees. Would the community partly match their contribution by raising sufficient funds to pay for a full-time trained supervisor? This proposal was unanimously accepted by the persons present and, it turned out, was a very wise one. It brought the community together in a common task that was to take months of work and involve literally thousands of people; it continually reminded the community that their efforts had secured the project in the first place and were needed to ensure its success.

Another important point made at this meeting was that although the Parks Department welcomed the gift of the playground, it already had difficulty adequately maintaining existing park facilities. This problem is one that plagues most city administrations: capital construction is usually financed outside the operating and maintenance budget. While it is relatively easy to find money to build with (the sponsors of Lincoln Center raised over a hundred million dollars toward its construction), it is difficult to ask donors also to finance the perpetual expense of yearly maintenance. In our own case, the problem was resolved by the cooperation of the three sponsoring organizations.

Because of the experimental nature of the playground and the fact that increased use was expected, the Department of Parks agreed to provide improved maintenance; the foundation promised a small annual sum to replenish the sand and the play construction materials, and the mothers' organization pledged to seek contributions of paper, paints, and other supplies, in addition to raising funds to pay for full-time supervision. Thus, many and diverse persons felt personally responsible for the upkeep of the facility, and felt justified in expecting an equal commitment from the other interested parties. This is extremely important in a large city where people often feel no personal involvement in the lives of their fellow citizens or in the workings of the city administration.

During the course of planning there were many

These drawings, done during the course of planning, incorporated changes suggested at meetings with the community. The boat in the left-hand sketch was not installed in the end, since it was felt that the space should be left open. The slide at lower left in the second sketch was relocated, and an amphitheater was built in its place.

A detailed scale model of the final design was made for the community and also used for fund-raising purposes.

meetings, with a variety of local groups, at which the designs were discussed and evaluated, but the bulk of the work now shifted to the mothers' committee and their activities.

The composition of the community in which the Adventure Playground was to be built is rather special but common to large cities. It consists of upper-middle-class families living in well-kept apartment buildings backed by blocks of deteriorating housing populated by poor families — some of them newly arrived migrants to city life — and large numbers of isolated persons living in single-room-occupancy buildings. Everyone involved in the planning of the new playground — the city, the foundation, the architect, and the mothers' committee — was of one mind that it should be a force for bringing together all segments of the community. To this end, we attempted to let as many residents as possible know about the playground and to elicit any suggestions they might have regarding its design, as well as their active support. All announcements concerning the playground were printed in both Spanish and English, to reach the large Spanish-speaking population and to clearly show that the new playground was intended for the whole community.

The publicity and fund-raising were as well organized as a political campaign. The mothers' committee became incorporated as a nonprofit organization, ensuring that any contributions made to it would be tax deductible. The neighborhood was divided into blocks and buildings, and responsibility for each section was assigned to one person. People were approached in a door to door canvass, usually by a person who lived in their building and therefore knew many of the residents. The new playground became the subject of wide interest, and television and newspaper coverage increased the pride and participation of the community. Thousands of reprints of the newspaper articles were obtained and used to acquaint people with the project. Donations were also solicited by mail, with a reprint and letter going to individuals and organizations on a mailing list compiled by the committee. The committee also contacted groups active in the community — local political clubs, churches, synagogues, businesses, a community center — and made slide presentations to many of them.

Since children, not adults, were to be the primary clients of the new facility, I made similar slide presentations at the local public schools. First I showed the existing playground, then drawings and a model of what was planned. I talked to the children, who ranged in age from about six to nine years old, in simple (but adult) language, concentrating on the specific items that would be included and pointing them out on the screen: each new item brought forth "Oohs" from the audience. At the end of the presentation, which lasted less than twenty-five minutes, questions were invited, and the children responded enthusiastically.

One day, about a year and a half later, I was visiting the playground, when an eight-year-old boy approached me and the following conversation took place:

"Hello!"
"Hello."
"I know who you are!"
"You do?"
"Yes, you're the architect, and you came to my school and showed us pictures!" (big grin)
"You're right!" (big grin)
"G'bye."
"G'bye."

Children playing during the construction of the playground.

Various events were held to raise funds and keep the community involved. A benefit film program raised almost one third of the entire goal. A large commercial movie house in the neighborhood allowed the use of its facilities without charge on a Saturday morning before the normal operating hours. The films selected were of special interest to children, but the parents, who would also have to sit through the showing, were considered too. (In many large cities, films may be borrowed at no cost from libraries or museums, or rented from film-rental agencies at a nominal cost.) The tickets were inexpensive enough to be within reach of the entire community — it was felt that selling a large number of low-priced tickets was preferable to selling a few expensive ones. As a result, among the many purchasers were persons who otherwise might not have donated to the fund.

Shortly before construction was to begin, a picnic was held at the existing playground. Local merchants were persuaded to donate food, soft drinks, and all the other ingredients of a picnic. These were sold, at nominal cost, at booths set up and staffed by volunteer mothers, fathers, Boy Scouts, Girl Scouts, and assorted other children from the neighborhood. At other booths visitors could buy used books or have their picture taken — the atmosphere was that of a miniature fair. A well-known television celebrity donated her services and led a sing-along program for the younger children; later, a rock band of eleven- and twelve-year-olds plugged their instruments into a lamppost, and the Sunday afternoon was enlivened by sounds that attracted hundreds of admiring youngsters. In all, over 2,000 persons attended, and several thousand dollars were raised. Although construction had not yet begun, the new playground already had become a part of the community life.

Construction

Contractors for most city construction projects are selected by public bidding — a time-consuming procedure in which the lowest bidder must be awarded the work. While this arrangement is reasonable when public funds are being disbursed, there is a way that private donations can be channeled into city-supported projects with a minimum of red tape.

The Department of Parks creates a special account to receive donations, and the donor stipulates the use of his gift — in this case, the playground. The donor hires the architect, and preliminary designs are prepared. After the Parks Department approves the drawings and specifications (which are subject to approval again when the details have been worked out), the architect obtains bids for the work. The donor and architect then select the contractor, and the donor deposits the amount of the bid plus the architect's fees in the special account. The architect is responsible for the supervision of the entire job and for the authorization of periodic payments to the contractor. When the contractor requests payment, the architect confirms that the work performed conforms to the request and authorizes the Parks Department to pay the contractor from the special account. The Parks Department issues payment, retaining 10 percent of it until final approval of the job. When the work is completed, the Parks Department, architect, and contractor together make a final inspection, and, as soon as any outstanding minor items are resolved, the Parks Department accepts the work and final payment is made.

In New York City this procedure has become

Part of the textured concrete peripheral wall completed.

The "bumpy" slide completed.

standard for park projects financed by private donors, and it has many advantages. The Parks Department assumes liability for the work, relieving the donor of this responsibility. The contractor is not only assured of payment but receives it more promptly than is possible under ordinary city contracts. Finally, the Parks Department is freed from the public bidding procedure and the equally lengthy process of preparing contracts for city work, and its over-worked staff can devote needed time to planning and supervising the capital construction and maintenance projects financed with public funds.

The construction process is one of the most fascinating things that a child (or an adult) can see in a city. Both boys and girls play with blocks, pails and shovels, miniature dump trucks and bulldozers, and other construction toys at some time in their childhood. In a society where many people do the kind of work that produces no visible (to children) end result, construction provides an especially good example of how the efforts of a number of men result in an appreciable change in the environment. During the course of the construction, I conducted several impromptu

tours of the construction with parents and children. I explained what the various elements were and what they would look like when the work was finished. I also asked the children to try out some of the structures and tell us what they thought; parents, too, were asked to comment. In this way, several structures were altered before the playground was completed.

Even the workmen, who alternated between very vocal objections to unusual elements and pride in their craftsmanship, became involved in the work, sometimes with unexpected results. In one instance the plans called for a curved wall to be made by pouring concrete into a form built with strips of grainy lumber of different widths and thicknesses. I intended that the boards be arranged in a random pattern so the concrete would have a lively, varied texture instead of the usual smooth finish. The workmen's innate sense of order would not let them arrange the boards at random, so they developed an elaborate system for placing the boards to make a symmetrical pattern. I overcame my mild outrage at seeing the design altered and congratulated the men for their ingenious plan. They subsequently felt free to use their initiative, and were extremely helpful

in devising solutions to other, more difficult problems.

One day I found the carpenters standing around a large slide, muttering to each other and shaking their heads, This slide — suggested to me by a little boy — was the "bumpy" slide. It had a wide track with three large bumps, and it was fairly steep, since it was intended for older children. The carpenters called me over, and one of them climbed up to demonstrate the problem personally. After a moment's hesitation, he slid down, revealing a spectacular feature of the design. As he went over the first bump, he sailed into the air and, flying completely over the second bump, landed noisily on the third. After he picked himself up from the sand at the base of the slide, we had a lengthy discussion regarding the forces of gravity, bumps, and the human anatomy. The result was a minor modification, and the slide thereafter lived up to everyone's expectations.

Modifications were made throughout the period of construction and afterwards, as the actual use of particular structures suggested alterations. The flagpole, for example, was included in the plans because a member of the mothers' committee had designed a playground flag, which was to be raised and lowered by the children under the watchful eye of the supervisor. The children soon tired of this activity, however, and one day they fastened the rope to someone's belt and hoisted him up the flagpole. A flagpole with adequate safeguards might someday be designed for this purpose, but since our flagpole was not, a lock had to be installed to prevent other experimentation with the rope.

Supervisors

As mentioned earlier, the mothers' committee agreed to raise funds for a full-time supervisor for the playground, and several members undertook the task of finding a qualified person. The requirements included several years' experience, a genuine enthusiasm for children, and the physical stamina required for a demanding outdoor job. Following the lead of the European adventure playgrounds, the mothers sought an adult who would provide assistance when the children requested it, but allow them the option of playing by themselves. (In Eng-

land the title "leader" is used, as it avoids the connotation of directing that "supervisor" has.) In other words, a supervisor should possess the good qualities of a parent without the parent's emotional stake in the children's performance.

The mothers eventually decided to hire two people — a woman to work in the morning, when the playground would be filled primarily with young children, and a young man to work in the afternoon, when older children come to play after school. In addition, the local community center obtained federal funds for a program to provide four trainees who would work under the direction of the two regular supervisors.

The problems of liability and insurance that would be posed if the mothers' committee employed the supervisors were avoided by another agreement with the Parks Department. The committee interviewed the applicants and selected the supervisors, who were then actually hired by the Parks Department and paid from a special account. This meant that the staff would be sensitive to the needs of the

community, while the city assumed the administrative burden, which it was better qualified than the community to handle.

The Design

Any specific design is the outcome of general criteria applied to a particular situation. The starting point must be some kind of unifying concept — a structure or framework through which the abstract ideas and the concrete realities are reconciled.

The site of the Adventure Playground was an old playground — a barren expanse of pavement relieved only by a water spray and the usual seesaws, swings, and slides. The fence around this area and the benches inside the fence were in good condition, as were the water supply and drainage facilities, and there were eight healthy trees, which provided just the right amount of shade. To keep within the budget of $85,000 for the construction, as much as possible of the existing playground was utilized. In the final design, the fence and benches, the two existing entrances, the plumbing, and all the trees were retained, and

Plan of the playground

1 Entrance
2 Entrance Tower
3 Maze
4 Tree Houses
5 Pyramid
6 Splashing Pool
7 Water Channel
8 Wading Pools
9 Table
10 Amphitheater
11 Climbing Poles
12 Slide
13 Volcano
14 Tunnel
15 Concentric Mounds (Crater)
16 Tree Pit
17 Tool Shed
18 Boat (not installed)

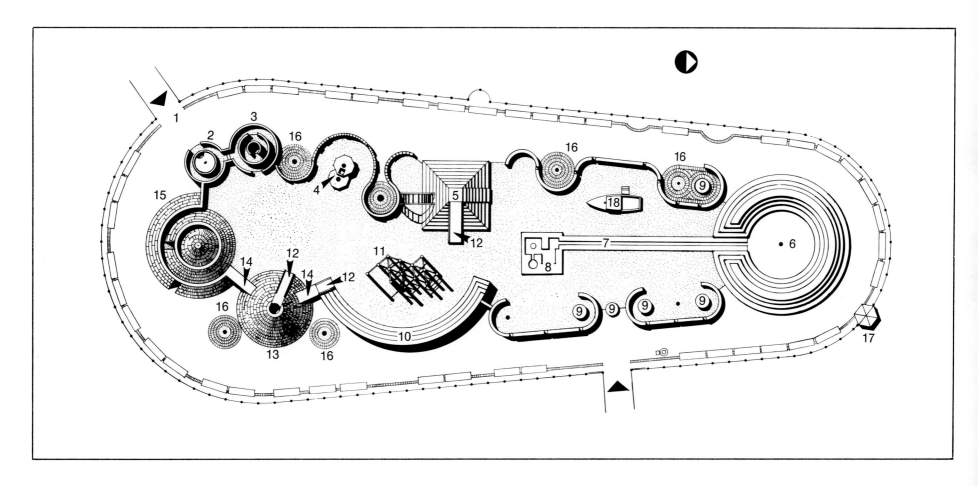

a new use was found even for the cobblestones from the old pavement.

The concept that provided the basis of the design was that of a group of small, varied, and related elements surrounding a large central space. This would allow a child to choose among a number of different activities and places while feeling always that he was part of a larger group. The different elements were linked together to permit movement from one to another and to enclose the central space to which all related. The linked structures thus form a sort of wall that defines the physical boundaries of the children's area. In their variety of size and function, these structures offer a full range of choice — from quiet, individual play to active undertakings involving groups of children, and from simple activities to more complex ones by a series of manageable steps. In this way, the older children provide models for the younger ones, but the initiative remains with the individual.

A further consideration was that the playground would function six days a week for most of the year as a supervised playground

and for the remaining time as an unsupervised playground. When the supervisor was present, construction materials, art supplies, games, and toys would be distributed and a full program of organized activities would be carried out, while for several months a year and on Sundays (the most crowded day), the equipment would not be available.

As a result, the playground is composed of two zones, each intended primarily for a specific kind of activity. The south half of the playground is designed for physical activities, including running, jumping, sliding, climbing, tunneling, balancing, and so on, and the north half of the site is designed for digging, building, painting, and playing with water. This different emphasis is carried through in the use of different surface materials — in the physical area sand, a soft cushion to fall and jump on; in the other area stabilized gravel, an ideal building material and a base firm enough to build on. (Stabilized gravel is a mixture of a sandy gravel and clay, which form a substance that has some of the advantages of both materials. It remains firm in dry weather and does not blow away, yet it does not become too soft

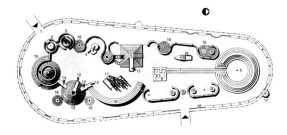

and muddy in rainy weather, and it drains rapidly.) It is important to note that there is a great deal of overlapping in possible activities. Both areas are designed to allow both kinds of activities to some extent, and there is no attempt to make the children conform to the designer's preconception. The idea is simply to make it more convenient and fun to do certain things in certain areas, with the hope that children will discover the qualities of all kinds of activities through their own experience.

Facing the main entrance (1) to the playground is a low entrance tower (2) that provides a gateway for the children — but not for the adults, since it is small enough to make their passage inconvenient. (All the structures in the playground were designed so that adults can, if necessary, enter, but they must stoop, wriggle, or climb a little to do so.) In this way children and parents are separated naturally. The children can climb to the top of the tower from the inside or the outside to survey the playground before entering.

The path through the entrance tower leads into a simple maze (3) before the central play area is reached, so that the children can feel that

The maze that leads into the playground is occasionally used in ways never anticipated by the designer.

One of the tree houses.

they are entering into their own private world. The maze represents an exciting and mysterious challenge for the youngest children, while the older ones walk around on top of the walls or jump from wall to wall above the toddlers' heads. The tower and maze, which resemble a fortress, were designed to be used also for games of strategy, and are the scene of all kinds of cowboy-and-indian-type battles as well as short-range snowball fights.

Continuing from the maze, we come to one of the peripheral walls that link all the structures (except the climbing poles) and wind, in serpentine fashion, around several trees (16). These walls, low enough to see over, serve to enclose and define the children's areas and create a continuous path around the playground; adventurous children may walk around the entire circumference — a route of about 500 feet — without once touching the ground. This section of the wall is a semicircle of heavy timbers set on end and varied in height to provide both a change of material and a small obstacle for those who are circumnavigating the playground. Within the semicircle is a large, sand-surfaced area containing two tree houses (4), one low and one high. They consist of tree

trunks — sanded smooth, shellacked, and set into concrete footings — with simple wooden platforms erected around them. (The tree trunks were obtained free from the Department of Parks, which has a continuing supply as a result of a regular program of removing dead trees from the city's parks.) The low tree house is easily accessible by two- to four-year-olds, while the ladder to the higher one has its rungs set farther apart, so that only older children can climb it; the oldest climb yet higher on the tree trunk itself and jump down from it to the sand below.

The next element is a pyramid-shaped structure (5). Located between the two main areas of the playground, it functions as a part of both. Its sides are stepped, and a child who climbs to the top has the choice of sliding down the bumpy slide (which is wide enough for two or three children to use simultaneously), standing around and watching until he can muster the courage to try it himself, or changing his mind and descending by the steps with honor intact. The steps are also good seats, commanding a view of the entire playground.

The pyramid is hollow, and it forms the roof of

The first step of the pyramid is high enough to discourage very small children from climbing it. The slide (the "bumpy" one) is the steepest of the three slides in the playground and wide enough for three children to use at once.

The splashing pool, the pyramid (showing the entrance to the interior), and the wall connecting the two elements. The low cast-concrete cubes at intervals in the wall provide seats and footholds.

The wading pools. Parents and children alike take off their shoes. A low concrete cylinder in the middle of the deepest pool makes a convenient table, seat, or stepping stone.

a twenty-foot-square storage room entered through a hatch on one side. The room houses the first-aid kit, changing facilities for the supervisors, all the construction, art, and craft materials, and miscellaneous play equipment. There is no heat, but natural ventilation is provided by a continuous vent under the pyramid overhang at ground level. The room has electrical outlets for lights, and record players or radios are plugged in for special programs, but an outlet for general use is provided on a nearby lamppost. The shovels and rakes used by park maintenance personnel are stored in a tool shed (17), so that only the supervisors need have access to the pyramid interior. Children are not allowed in because the space is limited and because it cannot be watched by the supervisor working outside in the playground.

Between the pyramid and the next element is a curving concrete section of wall. This provides a support for construction materials and an easel for painting, as well as marking out a series of small areas for play. Within the curves outside the wall is another series of areas containing trees or low platforms, where toddlers can play just a few feet from their mothers.

A splashing pool (6) occupies the entire north end of the playground. It utilizes a water spray and drainage system from the old playground, but a stepped concrete ring was added around the spray. When the water is on, this ring separates the wet activities from the dry and provides seating for the children on the inside as well as parents on the outside. (When the water is off, the ring forms an amphitheater that can be used for quiet sitting, storytelling, puppet shows, and a variety of games.) In the old playground, the water was drained away immediately into the city storm sewer. Now this precious play material does not disappear so quickly. The water first collects in a channel just inside the concrete ring, then flows into a long channel (7). This version of the street gutters where children have so much fun is wide and made of nonslip concrete, so everyone can run up and down, splashing water in every direction. (In warm weather all the children and most of the mothers take off their shoes; many of the very young children take off everything.) The five- to eight-year-olds like to float things in the stream — leaves, sticks, paper boats, or plastic boats that are available from the supervisor: boat-racing is a favorite game. Older children try to dam the stream,

using their bodies or anything handy. While it is easy to stop the flow partially and build up the water level on the upstream side, the channel is wide enough so that it is very difficult to halt the flow completely. When this does happen, however, the water soaks harmlessly into the gravel. In the absence of water, the channel is used to roll things down or just to run in.

At the end of the channel are several shallow pools (8) ranging in depth from two to six inches. A little waterfall pours into them from the channel, providing an exciting end for boat races. The pools hold enough water to sit in and scoop up in pails, but they are not deep enough to require a lifeguard or even anxious attention from parents. Next to splashing, the favorite pastimes here seem to be collecting water for various construction projects taking place in the sand, and throwing sand in — apparently to try to fill up the pools or simply to watch the sand disappear into the water. The pools were designed to accommodate all these uses. Water drains out of them only when they are full, from the overflow spouts at the highest level the water reaches. Thus, most of the sand falls to the bottom from which it can be removed before the cleanout drains at the

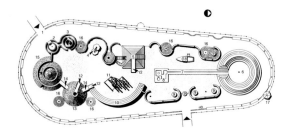

The volcano, with a small slide and a medium-sized one. The protective rail at the top of the mound was not in the original design of the structure, but is useful when a lot of children crowd the top.

bottom are opened. This system notwithstanding, a lot of sand finds its way into the drains over the course of a season, and this is trapped in a catch basin outside the playground. Several bushels of sand yearly are removed from it and discarded by the Parks Department.

To the east of the channel, flanking and bridging a small entrance to the playground, is another section of concrete wall like that described previously. Next is a crescent-shaped amphitheater (10). This area was intended for sitting and playing when not in use as a theater. In front of it, providing convenient supports for mounting simple stage scenery, are the climbing poles (11).

Made of redwood with steel rungs, the climbing poles represent some improvement over the traditional monkey bars. From a purely aesthetic standpoint, the smooth redwood is more pleasant to touch and far better looking than a steel jungle gym. The height of the poles varies, as does the spacing of the rungs — the rungs at the bottom are spaced more closely together. This allows young children to use the climbing poles just like the older ones, but their limited reach keeps them on the safe

lower levels. The poles are completely surrounded by sand to cushion jumps and falls. Falls are extremely infrequent, however, because hand- and footholds are large and close together. A knotted nylon rope is attached to the highest rung — and anchored on a low rung — so that it can be used for climbing but not for swinging. When supervised activities are going on, the poles can also serve as a big easel: large sheets of brown paper are stapled to them, forming a number of separate panels where children can paint.

At the south end of the amphitheater is a slide (12) — the smallest of the three in the playground. This slide is very attractive to two-, three-, and four-year-olds just beginning their sliding career and is completely ignored by the older children. It can be reached by climbing the low steps of the amphitheater or by way of an inclined ramp around the adjacent volcano.

The volcano (13), a mound surfaced with granite cobblestones, is the most complex structure in the playground. It can be approached in several ways: from the two adjoining elements; by means of a tunnel that goes all the way through the volcano (and has a vertical

The concentric mounds, or crater. In the background is the tunnel leading from the interior of the volcano. The beginning of the ramp around the volcano can also be seen.

Modular toys are stored inside the pyramid and distributed by the playground supervisor. The panels are made of plywood notched to fit together. For toddlers there are small wood blocks, nesting boxes, and a smaller version of the modular panels (opposite page, below).

84

The path around the playground, lined with benches, is used by parents, children, and passers-by.

tunnel and ladder leading to the summit); along a gently inclined ramp circling the mound; or directly up the sides, where recessed cobblestones serve as hand- and footholds. Recessed steps rather than projecting ones were used because they allow for a harmless slide to the sand below in the event someone does slip or fall. (At the rear of the volcano, where there is asphalt paving, the ramp forms an intermediate level to break falls.) For those who reach the top, there is a safe vantage point, protected by a handrail, from which children can look around or descend via a medium-sized slide or any other route they wish.

The tunnel (14) underneath the volcano and the shaft that leads to the summit are great favorites. The first rung of the ladder is high enough to prevent the youngest children from making the six-foot climb, and the area under the ladder is padded with rubber safety surfacing. All the entrances to the tunnel (there are two at each end, plus the one at the top) are big enough for an adult to use if necessary, but the effort required effectively keeps most parents out. The tunnel floor is pitched to prevent water accumulation when it rains, and there

are no blind corners to encourage use of the tunnel as a toilet.

At the south end of the playground are the concentric mounds (15), often called the "crater." Like the other structures, this is used in different ways by children of different ages. The youngest play in the sand between the inclined cobblestone walls and make their way to the center mound by way of small openings. Older children climb up and over the walls to reach the center, and the most intrepid leap from wall to wall.

We thus complete our circuit of the playground and its facilities. Two portions of the playground remain to be mentioned: the open central space and the area between the main structures and the outer fence. The first is full of children running from place to place — or just running — and others playing in the sand or building with construction materials. The second, paved with asphalt, is used by adults and children both. It provides a hard-surfaced path for baby carriages and tricycles and other wheeled toys, as well as a promenade for parents and passers-by. This traffic does not interfere with the children playing in the central area, and the number of people and obstacles on the route limits movement to a safe speed.

Evaluation

The Adventure Playground has now been in use for several years, and it is possible to analyze how its use differs from that contemplated by the persons involved in its design. Such evaluations are seldom undertaken, usually because the time is lacking, with the result that designers often repeat their mistakes.

As in the observation of birds and animals in nature, the goal is to sit very quietly and patiently until one becomes a part of the surroundings — and thereby invisible to the children — and pay attention to what is happening. (When an adult intrudes with questions, children are abruptly pulled back into the world of adult expectations, and the answers often bear little relation to the way they really feel. I once asked a little boy what he liked best about the Adventure Playground and he unhesitatingly answered, "Me!")

It was convenient that a typical "asphalt desert" playground stood next to the Adventure Playground for over a year — until it was rebuilt as a companion playground. The children thus had the option of voting with their feet, and most of them consistently voted to play in the Adventure Playground. The number of children using it simultaneously has been surprising: sometimes as many as 300 children and as many adults have filled the playground; in the old one the presence of twenty-five would have been notable. During the spring and fall, five to ten school buses arrive every weekday bringing nursery, kindergarten, and first-grade classes from schools as far as thirty miles away. (The teachers who bring these groups supervise their activities, and this helps to keep things operating smoothly.) The playground is often overcrowded on weekends, when families come from many parts of the city. The overcrowding, of course, reflects the demand for more well-designed playgrounds. (Many of the "local" mothers avoid the playground at these times; some of them have expressed their chagrin at finding the project so successful. The initial efforts to involve the community were more effective

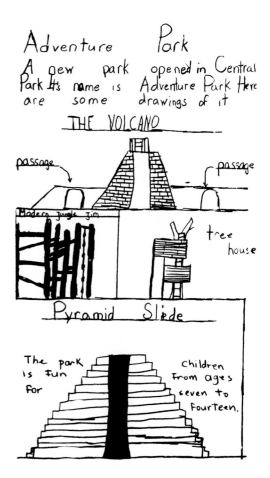

Adventure Park

A new park opened in Central Park. It's name is Adventure Park. Here are some drawings of it

THE VOLCANO

passage

passage

Modern Jungle Jim

tree house

Pyramid Slide

The park is fun for

children from ages seven to fourteen.

than anyone expected, and have resulted in a sense of private ownership among the mothers and their children. This phenomenon has caused no real problems and is certainly preferable to lack of concern.)

Despite an average attendance ten times that of the old playground, there have been no serious accidents at the Adventure Playground (in contrast, at the small playground next door there were at least two, including a brain concussion that resulted in the removal of the jungle gym). There are fewer falls, and most of them are cushioned by the soft sand, while scraped knees have been reduced to a minimum. Occasionally, a very bold toddler manages to climb the pyramid and go down the large slide, landing in the sand with a jolt. This usually happens because a mother assumes that since the playground is much safer than before, she need no longer keep an eye on her child. Although every structure is designed to discourage children from using parts that are beyond their ability, there are always children who will attempt more than they can handle, and no amount of design can prevent this. No playground can prevent a child from being hurt

(and if it protected him from upset completely, it would convey the very misleading impression that he has nothing to fear from his environment); what it can do is prevent the serious injuries that occur in the typical playground.

The children's use of the different elements in the Adventure Playground seems to follow no pattern — their interest shifts constantly from one activity to another. However, some things are clearly more popular than others. In order of use, the most popular elements are: the pyramid; the splashing pool, water channel, and wading pools (in the summer when the water is on); the volcano and tunnel complex; and the tree houses. That fact that some elements are used more than others is not in itself a criticism (more people go to baseball games than ping-pong tournaments) — the problem is overcrowding. Since all the elements involved except the splashing pool are in the same general area, near the middle of the playground, there is a greater concentration of activity here than at the two ends. One solution for this situation might be to apply the principle that has long been followed in the design of shopping centers: the facilities used most are

placed at opposite ends of a mall, with specialty stores in between. This generates movement between the main drawing points, and the intermediate stops get the benefit of the increased traffic. To adapt this to a playground, the elements of proved popularity would be spaced out, with areas for other activities between them. However, there should always be some corners where a child can get away from the surrounding activity.

The operation of the playground as a whole has yielded another very important lesson for the design of future facilities: namely, that sand, like water, flows to the lowest point. The process is a slow one but nevertheless results in the loss of a great deal of sand, not only through water drains, as already noted, but also onto the pavement outside, through openings in the walls around the sand areas. This suggests that a reservoir for sand should be designed exactly like one for water. Raising openings in surrounding walls will eliminate most of the problem, but a system of steps probably would be a better solution. Since children love to transport sand from one place to another, steps would provide an intermediate zone where they could dump it and from

which it would work its way back to the original reservoir.

The same problem exists — although to a lesser degree — with the water. A dozen children filling pails from the pools and dumping them on the surrounding gravel for hours finally taxes the drainage capacity of the ground and creates a puddle. The children love this, but from the adults' point of view, an intermediate zone from which the water could flow back into the pools is preferable.

Since another problem occurs where the sand meets the gravel, we can formulate the basic observation that a problem arises at every point where two different materials meet — sand and pavement, sand and gravel, gravel and water. The zone of meeting must be designed to reduce this (it cannot be eliminated entirely); steps or a system of double barriers (like locks along a waterway or double doors at the entrance to a building) seem suitable, since they allow children to play with and mix different materials but provide a way to separate them again.

The sand itself — white beach sand — has

been satisfactory, primarily because drainage is adequate. Rain cleans most of the dirt from it, but refuse has to be picked up. The supervisors have cleverly enlisted the children's help for this task, thus not only removing the paper, bottles, and other trash to the receptacles provided and emptied by the Parks Department, but also discouraging the youngsters from adding to it. Maintenance is very important. There is no such thing as a playground that requires no cleaning, but few people will litter a clean place, while a dirty one only encourages the accumulation of more dirt.

The nontransportable materials in the playground have withstood use well. The exposed concrete and cobblestones have required no maintenance at all. The dark stain finish of the wood surfaces is worn off in spots by countless feet and hands, and a new coat of stain is applied yearly. This is an inexpensive and simple process, since stain penetrates directly into the wood and the old finish does not have to be removed, as is the case with paint.

The playground was designed to provide many places outside the walls where young children could play near their parents and, on the

assumption that the toddlers would prefer it, away from older children. Observation of the under-five-year-olds in action shows that the reverse is closer to the truth — most of them choose to play in the sand inside the walls, as close as possible to the major activities. They sit for hours, apparently enjoying the frenzied movement around them. The solution might be to provide protected areas adjacent to the centers of activity rather than removed from them, and this fits nicely with the shopping center approach of distributing areas for a variety of activities between the points of greatest concentration.

Although the ingenuity of children was planned for relatively well, that of parents was underestimated. They have taken over entire sections of the peripheral walls, as well as the amphitheater near the climbing poles, which now serves as a seating area for them as well as a storage place for shoes. The presence of sand induces all the children to remove their shoes, and many mothers do the same, thus circumventing one of the obstacles intended to keep them out of the play area. However, most of these trespassers are the parents of very young children, which accounts for their desire

to stay nearby. Another consideration overlooked in the design is that fathers will go almost anywhere to take a picture of their offspring. While the children might prefer to exclude adults altogether, the designer must take the parents' needs into account as well, and the best solution is probably a compromise — to make some areas easier for parents to enter and others much more difficult.

The reception that teen-agers have given the Adventure Playground is extremely interesting. This group presents one of the most complex problems related to playgrounds. The sheer number of youngsters and parents in the Adventure Playground throughout the daytime discourages most teen-agers from using it then; in addition, adolescents are reluctant to be identified with the younger children. But at 10:00 P.M., when the gates are locked, teen-agers climb over the fence and play, by themselves and unobserved. They apparently find enough challenges to their skill and nerve to keep them engrossed, but the fact remains that they basically are excluded from the playground, and this could invite vandalism in retaliation.

This possibility might be avoided by setting

aside the evening hours for their exclusive use. A playground can be used for dances, talent shows, music programs, plays, athletic contests, or just discussions. Teen-agers make noise, but providing them with a reasonable period of time to use the playground, adequate facilities, and, if necessary, sympathetic leadership might go a long way toward assuring them that their needs are being considered too.

Alternatively, a section of the playground might be reserved at all times for teen-agers. The skills they possess can and should be utilized and challenged fully by the equipment and supervised projects. (This system is used successfully in many British adventure playgrounds.) Basketball courts and ball fields are usually available in our cities, but areas for imaginative play — and facilities for girls — are almost never provided. There are many things that adolescent girls might do in a well-designed and properly supervised playground, including cooking, painting, and a variety of physical activities, which girls enjoy just as much as boys. Teen-age play has too often been limited to team sports for boys, while the creative and constructive activities, which are as much fun and much richer in their educational content, have been slighted.

90

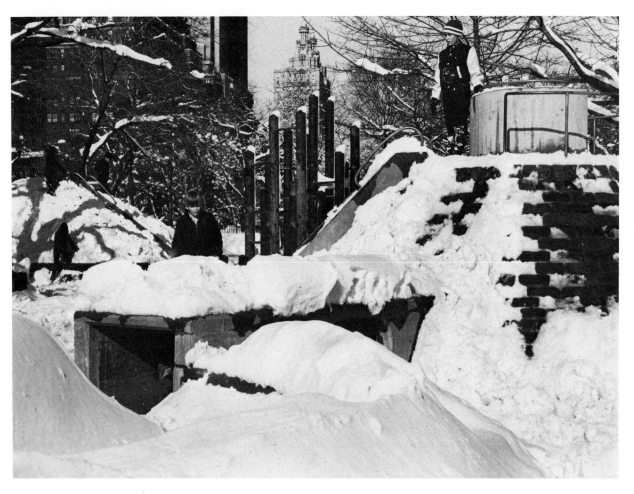

Conclusion

The Adventure Playground mothers' committee has stayed together, and currently organizes two annual events — a picnic at the playground and a theater or film benefit — to raise funds to pay the supervisors for the following year. The committee has also assisted in other playground projects, among them the construction of the new small playground next door. The foundation that sponsored the Adventure Playground has also remained actively involved in its operation and maintenance, making periodic contributions to replenish the sand or provide additional play materials. The history of the Adventure Playground indicates that city agencies, community organizations, and private sponsors can work together toward the common goal of creating play facilities based on the real needs of children. It shows also that children respond to these efforts on their behalf and express their approval in the most natural way they know — simply by using what is created for them, and enjoying it.

a portfolio of recent playgrounds

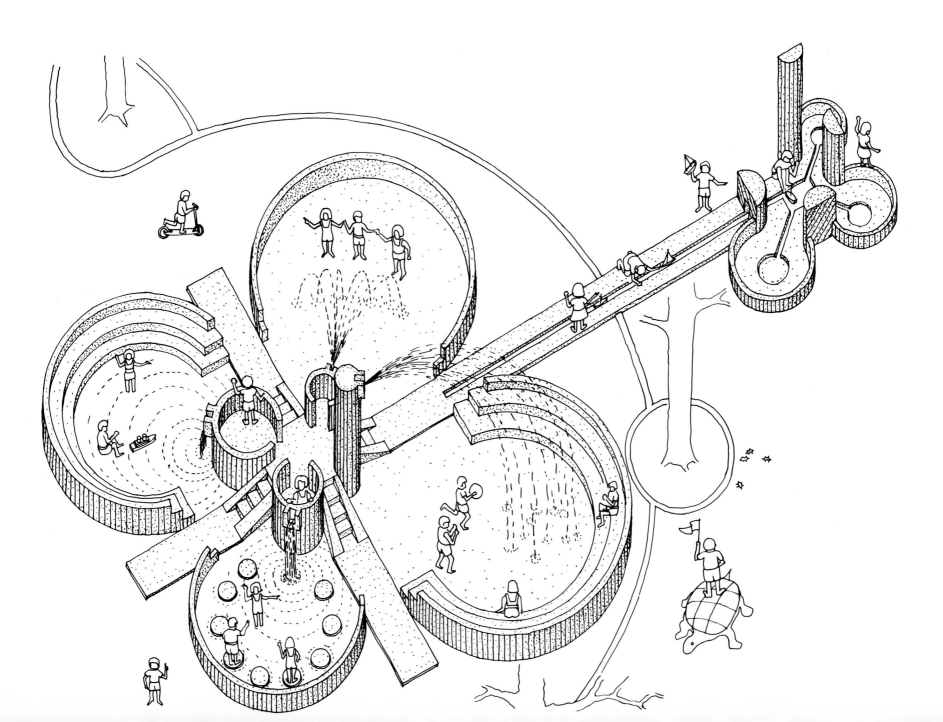

West 81st Street Playground, Central Park: N.Y.C.
Richard Dattner, Architect

This play area, built on a portion of an existing playground, is used for water play in warm weather and for climbing and hide-and-seek games in cold weather. The original design (opposite) included a water channel, which was eliminated to lower costs; the circular forms were modified to octagons to make construction of the concrete formwork easier.

Each of the four towers with its corresponding pool provides a different experience with water, ranging from the fine spray from the highest tower to a stream from the lowest, which pours into a shallow wading pool. The water is nowhere more than a few inches deep and drains into an accessible catch basin under the concrete platform. The pool floors are red, nonslip concrete. The sprays are recessed into the concrete: children can still play with the water, but the fixtures are relatively protected from accidental or intentional damage.

Raised walks between the towers separate the pools and allow children and adults to watch without getting wet.

Eiseman Nursery Playground: New York City
Michael Altschuler, Designer

This compact playground replaced a little-used backyard and shows what can be done with a very limited budget. Clockwise from lower left (below) are: planting pot and bench, playhouse, painting corner with easels, movable blocks on wood dowels, sandbox with plastic funnels, rows of chimes and bells, and an arch with a distorting mirror inside. The sun in the center was painted by volunteers; parents worked with the designer on the whole project.

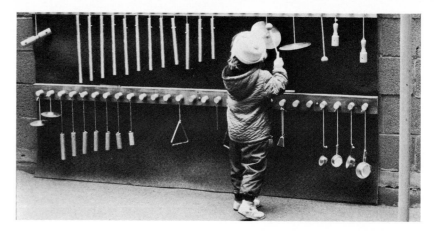

St. Barnabas House Playground: New York City
Robert Nichols, Architect

A vacant lot was transformed into an adventure playground with cast-off and donated materials. The seats were obtained from an old theater; old tires were bolted together to form a piece of equipment that can be rolled, climbed into, and bounced on, and the wastebaskets were painted in brilliant colors by the staff and the children. The cable spools are sturdy enough to support the weight of several children. In construction behind the cable spools is a tunnel — a row of oil drums with ends removed set in a channel to be covered with a mound of earth.

Plan of the playground

(1) Manipulative Wall   (2) Musical Screen   (3) Fence
(4) Play Tables   (5) Commando Net   (6) Docks
(7) Umbrellas/Seats   (8) Stream   (9) Boat Building Desk
(10) Boat   (11) Debarked Tree   (12) Stave Pipe Tunnel
(13) Bridges   (14) Gangplanks   (15) Mounds
(16) Tunnel   (17) Tree Trunk Slide   (18) Stepping Logs
(19) Step Tree Trunks   (20) Log Building Area
(21) Chalkboard   (22) Paint on Alcove   (23) Tree House
(24) Tepee   (25) Playhouse/Slide   (26) Rocking Boat
(27) Sandbox   (28) Seat   (29) Water Tap   (30) Hedge
(31) Pine Trees   (32) Milking Stools   (33) Shoe Storage

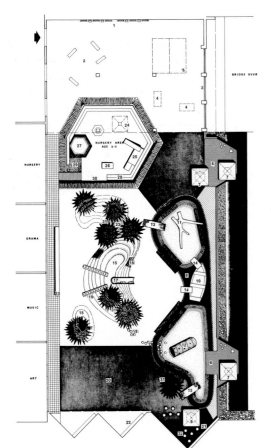

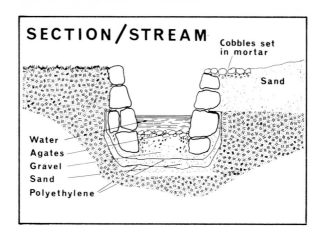

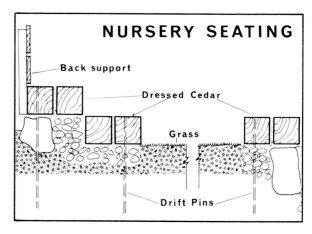

SECTION/STREAM

Cobbles set in mortar
Sand
Water
Agates
Gravel
Sand
Polyethylene

NURSERY SEATING

Back support
Dressed Cedar
Grass
Drift Pins

Children's Creative Centre, Expo 67: Montreal
Cornelia Hahn Oberlander, Landscape Architect

This adventure playground, used in conjunction with adjoining demonstration classrooms and supervised by experienced teachers, was part of the Canadian pavilion at Expo 67. Parents were not allowed in the play area, although they could watch the activity from an upper level of the pavilion.

A small rowboat (see opposite page) moored in a shallow stream was one of the young visitors' favorite playthings: the thrill of being afloat is not diminished by the fact that the boat cannot really go anywhere. Although the water was not deep and the boat could not be tipped over, a supervisor was on hand and always should be around such facilities. Next to the rowboat was a tunnel made from a wooden water tank with cut-out viewing portholes. In the adjacent building area were logs (supplied by a manufacturer of prefabricated log cabins) that were large enough to make good-sized structures. A tree house (also see opposite) was built around — but not supported by — three living trees.

A wooden ladder, a rope ladder, a notched timber, and a brass pole provided several means of ascending to and descending from the tree house. The notched timber (below) was inexpensive and presented the children with a new challenge.

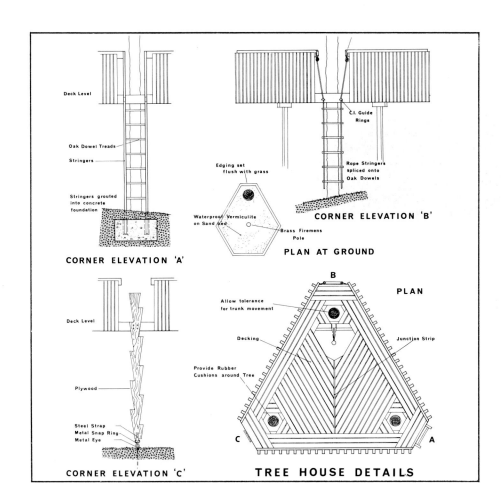

CORNER ELEVATION 'A'

PLAN AT GROUND

CORNER ELEVATION 'B'

CORNER ELEVATION 'C'

TREE HOUSE DETAILS

Park and Playground: Highland Park, Michigan
Richard Dattner, Architect

A community recreation area has been created by closing off a street. There are play areas for toddlers and for older children, and a sitting area for adults around a sunken amphitheater that doubles as a splashing pool. The wooden trellis structures provide shade and are equipped with plastic globes for lighting.

Riverdale Neighborhood House Playground: N.Y.C.
Richard Dattner, Architect

An addition to an existing building, this building and playground are designed to serve many recreational uses. The building itself, as well as the space outside it, is utilized. On the roof are tennis and handball courts in the summer — an ice-skating rink in the winter. The nursery-school classrooms on the lower level open onto a multi-use playground accessible to the community by a ramp (at far right in the sketch). The building is made part of the play experience: a blackboard, raised letters, and a clock are set into the wall; and play niches, a slide, and a brass pole for sliding are built into the ramp.

**Camp Hill Development: Borough of Nuneaton, England
Mary Mitchell, F.I.L.A., Landscape Architect**

A simple series of huge mounds surfaced in sprayed concrete adjoining a large pond makes an effective contrast to expanses of grass. The slide on the twenty-one-foot-high mound shown below is gentle enough for small children but long enough to make the ride interesting to older ones too. Additional slides on the mound might have shortened the waiting time at the top.

Children's Zoo: Rapperswil (Zurich)

The giant concrete whale with an eye made from a steel gear is large enough to become part of the landscape; a smaller version might have been merely a novelty object, providing a seat but not much more. Climbing ropes make the top accessible.

**Kingshurst Estate Playground: Birmingham, England
Mary Mitchell, F.I.L.A., Landscape Architect**

The concrete hillside with tree-trunk steps and a slide is more interesting than the steel climbing structure in the playground, and much safer.

De Anza Playground: Sunnyvale, California
Win Ng, Designer

A very attractive sculptural treatment with a variety of
textures. Water runs in the channel with the smooth
pebble bottom. Missing, however, is any way for children
to have an effect on the environment.

Twenty-seventh Street Playground: Kansas City, Mo.
Dale Eldred, Designer

This play facility uses only natural materials. The climbing structure behind the pool (below, left) consists of
four tree trunks stripped of their bark and set into concrete. Large rocks piled in a secure mound (below, right)
provide hand- and footholds for children climbing to the
forest of smooth tree trunks at the summit.

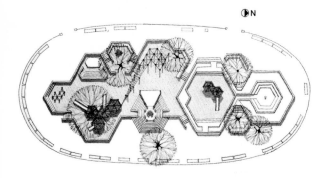

East 72nd Street Playground, Central Park: N.Y.C.
Richard Dattner, Architect

This facility (left and below, left) is to be built on the site of an old asphalt playground, and the design includes the existing trees and drainage system. In the south half of the playground are climbing poles for young children, a small amphitheater, a toddler area with climbing timbers, climbing poles (for older children) connected by a rope net to a series of tree houses and slides, and a cobblestone pyramid with a tunnel and a broad slide. At the north end of the playground is a splashing pool. Water from a central spray will collect in the channel around the pool, flow into the hexagonal channel around two more tree houses, and return to the pool to drain. Thus, the existing water pipe and drain are used, but the water travels a long route before draining away.

Garden Street Tot Lot: New Haven
New Haven Redevelopment Agency
Arthur Selbert, Designer

This facility (below, center) is one of the first of a number of small play areas to be developed on vacant lots by the City of New Haven.

Cable Ride: Sanbornton, New Hampshire
Haven Sanborn, Designer

Constructed from scrap machine parts and a cable from a well-drilling rig, this ride can be used by several children at one time. It carries them on a gentle 600-foot journey close to the ground. A rope is used to pull the rolling pulley back to the top of the slope.

Jacob Riis Houses Playground: New York City
Pomerance and Breines, Architects
M. Paul Friedberg & Assocs., Landscape Architects

This imaginative playground (right) replaces a formerly barren grass area inside a housing project. Areas for adults to sit in, and an amphitheater, are included nearby.

The Metropolitan Museum of Art Playground: N.Y.C.
Richard Dattner, Architect

Sketch for a playground to adjoin the Egyptian Wing of the Museum. In the center is a complex pyramid structure with slides, sand pits, and tunnels, and tree houses equipped with ladders, slides, and sliding poles are connected to two sides of the pyramid. From the splashing pool to the left of the pyramid water will flow in a channel to a smaller pool. The small square areas enclosed on three sides are for toddlers. The slide at top, right, is about 100 feet long and leads into the playground from an adjoining rock outcropping. The playground is also designed to introduce children to some aspects of ancient Egyptian culture. In the shaded areas on the right, sphinxes and other appropriate objects will be set into the sand. The benches and fence around the playground are from a previous facility.

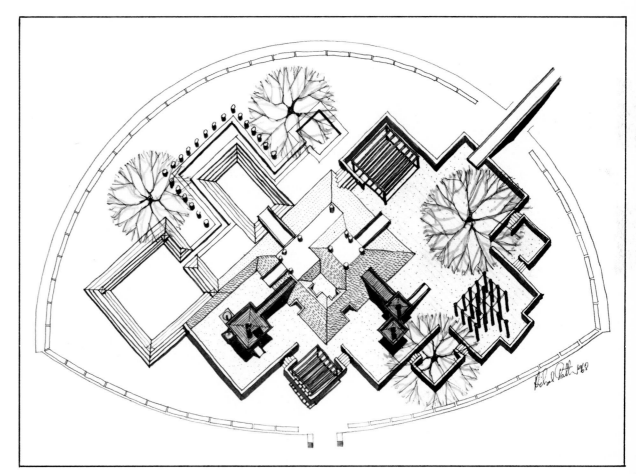

Lower Playground, Central Park: New York City
Richard Dattner, Architect

This small playground adjoining the Adventure Playground was designed for the young children who find
the neighboring facility too big or too busy. There is a
small, open playhouse with a slide: the upper level,
where the slide begins, is reached by means of a ladder.
Sand at the base of the ladder and the end of the slide
provides soft landing places. The lower level of the
playhouse can be used by children reluctant to climb the
ladder, and the timber foundation makes a low bench.
Seen behind the playhouse is a low concrete pyramid
that has a toddler-sized slide.

Concrete arches (below) form a gateway to the tricycle
track that winds its way around the entire playground.
Parents must duck down if they want to enter by this
route. The arches are low enough for agile youngsters
to get to the top, but very young ones cannot manage the
climb and play around the base.

**Howell Avenue School Playground: Valley Stream, N.Y.
Richard Dattner, Architect**

Sketch for a combined school and community playground built on a strict budget. All of the structures — designed to be constructed by the school maintenance staff — are supported on inexpensive wood poles. Clockwise from lower left are: a stage and amphitheater for outdoor classes, a rope net suspended over deep sand, an earth mound with concrete-pipe tunnels, a rope bridge linking two wooden platforms, climbing poles, a splashing pool (obscured by trees), and a water channel.

**Corona Avenue School Playground: Valley Stream, N.Y.
Richard Dattner, Architect**

Design for a companion facility to the Howell Avenue School playground. The area is protected and visually separated from a busy intersection by a fence and a tall hedge. The splashing pool at the right is used for ice-skating in the winter.

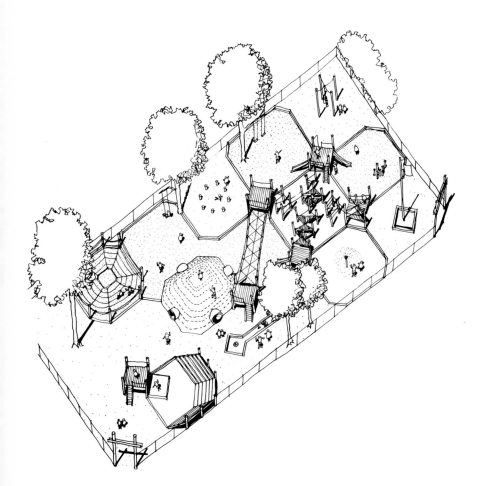

106

Heckscher Playground, Central Park: New York City
Richard Dattner, Architect

Design for a facility on the site of an old asphalt playground. The rock outcroppings are the favorite play spots
in the old playground, and this is reflected in the new
design. Instead of the single, unbroken expanse of pavement, three interrelated play areas are planned around
the central space (with flagpole). The section for young
children (at top, right, in the plan) will contain mounds,
pyramids, slides, climbing poles, an amphitheater, and
tree houses around an area of sand. The section for
older children and teen-agers (bottom) will utilize a large
rock outcropping for three long slides and include a
basketball court as well as swings and climbing equipment. The base of another outcropping (top, left) is a
wading pool within which two small spray pools are to be
built; portions of the rock will be smoothed for sliding,
and a tower overlooking the playground will be built at
the top. The chain-link fence that enclosed the old playground has been removed, but three gateways allowing
free entry will preserve some sense of enclosure for the
children. The new construction will be integrated with
the existing landscape as shown in the sketch (above).
The observation tower is at far left in the sketch and the
play area for older children at far right.

playgrounds for handicapped children 8

*To grow means to be divided into different
parts which move at different rates.*

— Erik H. Erikson

In the foregoing chapters we have considered
the requirements of normal children for play
facilities that engage their interest and imagination. Unfortunately, there are also many
children who, because of mental, physical, or
emotional handicaps, spend most of their life
in an institution. Their needs are greater than
those of normal children because they cannot
do as much for themselves, and a well-designed play environment is especially important to them.

In doing research for the design of play facilities for several institutions, I have had the
opportunity recently to observe handicapped
children at play. The most important result of
my study was the discovery that the play of
exceptional children is in most ways identical
to that of normal children. This is not to say
that handicapped children face no obstacles in
using a playground — depending on their
problems, they encounter various difficulties in
motion or perception, and some are so seriously disabled that most ordinary activities are
beyond their reach. But the primary fact remains valid: to the extent of their abilities, their
play follows the same patterns as that of
normal children; it serves the same function of

expanding their experience and understanding
of the world, and it affords them the same
potential for enjoyment and expression.

Once, during a visit to the children's rehabilitation unit of a large hospital, I met a six- or
seven-year-old boy who had been born without
arms or legs. A nurse was helping him to put
on artificial legs, and I was overwhelmed by
the tragedy of his circumstances. The hope
that he might use and enjoy a playground
seemed pathetically unrealistic. A few minutes
later I was walking outside, and he ran past
me, at full speed, followed closely by a group
of children in wheelchairs and on crutches. He
returned to talk to me and for the next hour
never left my side, subjecting me to a constant
stream of questions while he led me around
the hospital grounds to show me his favorite
places. Walking on the artificial limbs was very
tiring for him, so the nurse helped him back to
his room to rest, although he was reluctant to
stop playing. When he said good-bye, he did
not seem pathetic any more. The terrible fact
of his extreme impairment was less important
than the fact that he was a little boy like all
other little boys, with all the qualities and
needs that they possessed. The part of him

that needed nurturing was that part which was
normal, and common to all children. The difference between this courageous little boy and
them was the amount of extra help and attention he needed to assist him in his growth.

Children with special problems need specially
designed playgrounds, but — it cannot be
repeated too often — their essential requirements are the same as those of normal children. The environment in which they play must
respond to that part of them which is healthy
and capable, with help, of growth and development. In the following pages are outlined some
of the problems presented by disabilities of
various kinds and some of the ways in which
the designer can approach them. These examples are offered not so much for the specific
solutions they represent as to illustrate how a
play facility can further medical goals for
handicapped children. It should be noted that
physical, mental, and emotional problems often
overlap; for example, physical damage usually
brings with it impaired perception and emotional development as well. Children in institutions are faced with a series of problems that
must be dealt with simultaneously, and the
difficulties sometimes seem insuperable. But

**Vacation Camp for the Blind: Spring Valley, New York
Samton Associates, Architects
M. Paul Friedberg, Landscape Architect**

Handrails create a route around the entire camp. Curved
sections indicate a change in direction in the path, a
step, or a building.

Vacation Camp for the Blind: Spring Valley, New York
Samton Associates, Architects
M. Paul Friedberg, Landscape Architect

This simple and inexpensive structure is made entirely
of wood, and the ground below is surfaced with soft sand.

Design for a playground for physically handicapped
children (opposite page) converts a large yard into a
series of small spaces encircled by a continuous water
channel set in the top of a low wall. Clockwise from
bottom, left, the circular areas include: a raised sandbox
and planting bed under a fiber glass umbrella for shade;
a climbing tower with a slide; a sunken swimming pool
with stepped sides; a small amphitheater; and two sitting
areas connected by a bridge between two gently inclined
circular ramps. A path under the bridge leads into and
winds through the central area of the playground.

there are usually some abilities present that
can be encouraged or reinforced, and these are
the qualities toward which the major efforts of
any institution should be directed.

Physically Handicapped Children

The three goals of physical rehabilitation are to
arrest the deterioration of existing abilities; to
strengthen skills that are imperfectly developed
but capable of further growth; and to provide
alternate, compensatory skills to replace those
that are lacking or irreparably damaged. Thus,
a child with a motor problem might be encouraged to walk to build up his physical power
and coordination; for a child who cannot walk,
facilities that help him move around must be
provided. In both cases, as with normal children, the environment should present a series
of challenges to be mastered gradually.

Before a playground can be designed to serve
a specific group of handicapped children, the
medical staff who treats them should be interviewed to determine what activities are thera-
peutic and which constitute potential dangers.

Different kinds of disabilities require different
strategies of treatment, and doctors, physical
and occupational therapists, and nurses can
furnish the designer with a great deal of specific information.

The playground described here was designed
for the children's rehabilitation unit of a hospital in New York City. It is an intensive-care
residential facility for about thirty children,
many of whom go home to their parents on
weekends. The children have serious physical
disabilities, including paraplegia, brain damage, and impairment caused by cerebral palsy,
muscular dystrophy, and polio. Almost all
need some prosthetic device, and get around
only with the help of crutches, wheelchairs,
or wheeled beds. They range in age from four
to sixteen and are housed by sex in separate
wings, although they go to school (in the
building) and play together. The old outdoor
play area consists of some ancient swings,
which have been modified so that children
wearing leg braces can use them. In the summer, a portable pool is set up, and the children have to be lifted in and out of the water.
After a series of meetings with the staff, the

following design was evolved by the architect.

In structure, the playground is similar to the Adventure Playground described in Chapter 6. It consists of a number of defined areas for specific activities around a central unifying space, and sand and water are the primary play materials. However, some basic modifications were required to suit this concept to the needs of its users.

All children love sand, but it poses problems for children wearing prosthetic devices because it gets into the joints and interferes with movement. The sandbed is therefore raised so the children cannot walk in it but can play with it from wheelchairs and beds, as well as standing up. (Many of the children must play and even eat standing up.) A recess around the perimeter of this area allows children in wheelchairs to get close enough to play comfortably. In addition to sand, there is also an area that contains soil for planting and digging.

Water is abundant as well, and it has similarly been placed at waist height. It flows slowly in a continuous channel set into the top of a low concrete wall that circles the entire play-ground. The flowing water invites the children to drop in objects, which begin a floating journey around the playground and entice the children to follow, thus providing exercise. The edge of the water channel forms a continuous handrail to assist the children in walking or pulling themselves around. Water also can be carried in pails to the sand and soil, further inducement for physical activity. There is a shallow pool for wading. Leading to it are low steps for those children who can negotiate them, and there is also a chair on a boom for lowering and lifting those who cannot manage the steps. This lessens the physical exertion required by the staff and makes entering and leaving the pool fun; it also decreases the possibility of injuries.

Under trees are sitting areas, which can be used for storytelling, singing, and outdoor classes. One of these areas is equipped with electric outlets for radios or record players, and the entire playground can be illuminated for nighttime recreation and parties.

The playground is laid out so that wheelchairs and beds can be maneuvered around every part of it, including curved ramps, a bridge, and an underpass. There are handrails on both sides of all the passages. The experience of going over and under things is thus available in a simple way that most of the children can utilize. There are steps to encourage those who are able to practice mastering the operation of climbing and descending. In addition, there are small openings to peek through and mirrors and other interesting materials set into the surfaces to look at and touch. Overhead are bars by which the children may pull themselves along; set into the ground are games and directional signs.

The playground is surrounded by grass areas where the children can picnic, sit and read under a tree, or just roll around — the grass offers no problem to the operation of prosthetic devices. The trees and shelter within the playground give shade during hot weather, and canvas shelters can be erected for additional protection from both sun and rain.

Although the various structures are designed to suit the problems of the children, the end remains the same — to give the children the maximum range of experience, and to allow them so far as possible to control it.

Bird S. Coler Hospital Playground: New York City
Richard Dattner, Architect

These drawings show how the water channel, sandbox,
planting bed, bridge, and underpass path are made accessible to children with a variety of physical handicaps.

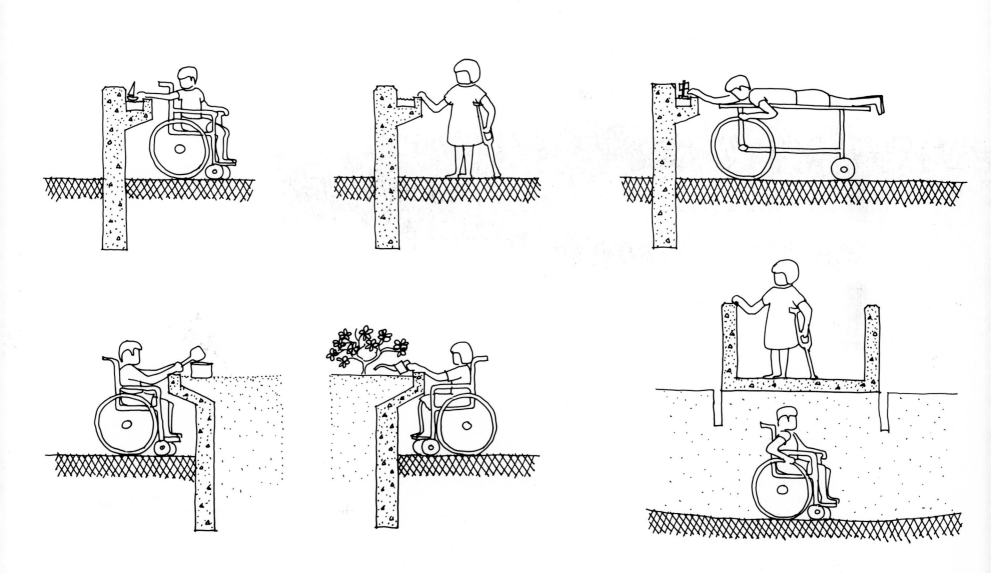

**Children's Day Treatment Center: New York City
Richard Dattner, Architect**

Two views of a model for a play area for emotionally disturbed children. The lightweight wood structures, which can be supported by the roof of an existing building, are designed to offer a series of activities for the youngsters. The canopy against one wall is to shade a sandbox and tables. The platform next to the timber climbing stockade will be equipped with a water spray and floored with nonslip rubber matting. The large main structure includes a slide and a wide, gentle ramp on one side and stepped seating on the other. Underneath it are a short tunnel and storage space for play materials. A wire mesh fence enclosing the entire rooftop is not shown.

Emotionally Disturbed Children

The difficulties faced by children with emotional and behavior disturbances are quite different from those of children with physical handicaps. Except in special cases, they have full use of their bodies; their problems involve perception and judgment. There are as many kinds of emotional disorders as there are physical disabilities, and play facilities must be designed to suit the individual situation.

Disturbed children may be unable to judge their limitations and undertake activities beyond their abilities, which can result in physical injury. They may confuse their wishes and fantasies with reality and consider themselves invulnerable; conversely, they may feel so vulnerable and unsafe that they hesitate to do anything for fear of instant injury or annihilation. Their perception of objects and spaces may be distorted — an open area can seem endless and an enclosed area confining. Many of these children have considerable difficulty in distinguishing where their bodies end and the rest of the world begins, and they may even be uncertain about their own existence under certain conditions. Some are extremely de-

structive; others are self-destructive.

Like all children, the emotionally disturbed need play facilities where they can learn about the physical world and themselves safely by means of graduated challenges and the opportunity to master new experience. However, it is particularly important that the environment be reassuring and unambiguous. Since reality often seems exaggerated to these children, extremes of all kinds should be avoided — no huge open spaces or long narrow tunnels, no steep slopes or very high places, no complicated mazes, and above all, no situations in which they lose the option of changing their mind.

For these children, the ordinary playground presents a series of dangerous and frightening conditions: bare expanses of hard pavement, treacherous seesaws and swings, and precariously high slides. Nothing yields to their efforts to control it, and failure is painful and potentially dangerous. Any problem that the equipment might present to a normal child is magnified disastrously for the disturbed one. It is interesting to note that groups from a school for emotionally disturbed children have

used the Adventure Playground in New York with no serious problems. Two or three teachers bring about a dozen children at a time for a few hours of closely supervised play. The water channel and the sand are among the most-used materials; with them the children can act out some of their feelings of aggression and hostility. The high structures, on the other hand, are generally avoided.

Several features make the Adventure Playground suitable for disturbed children. The various areas are manageable in size and well defined, giving reassurance to those who are confused about space. The children always have the choice of changing their mind if they become frightened. There is also an opportunity to watch other children mastering an activity from nearby, without having to undertake it immediately.

The design for a low-cost roof playground at a New York treatment center for disturbed children incorporates some of these features on a limited scale. The roof is enclosed completely by a high wire fence, both to prevent accidents and to foster a sense of security. The floor of hard quarry tile is covered with a soft, resilient,

all-weather material (rubber matting or nylon artificial grass). On this surface are a number of wooden structures light enough to be supported by the existing roof. These include a low, stepped ramp that can double as an amphitheater, a slide, a tower with a brass pole to slide down, an underpass (enclosed for only three feet), a low corral for climbing, a shaded area with table surfaces, and a sand box. The space under the stepped ramp and slide is utilized for storage of toys and other equipment. There is provision for a water spray for use in warm weather. These areas can be adapted for activities such as painting, working with clay, and other activities that serve as outlets for creative and expressive needs. This kind of design creates a varied potential for play and other supervised activities, while providing a safe environment.

The same qualities important in playgrounds for disturbed children are necessary in environments designed for disturbed adults. It does not seem farfetched to suggest that playgrounds might be designed for adults with severe mental disturbances, so they might safely learn about themselves and their physical environment.

Retarded Children

Many retarded children now receive treatment and special education at an early enough age so that they can lead productive, although limited, lives. Because of the enlightened modern practice of returning these least retarded children to the community, institutions are increasingly able to concentrate on caring for those who are severely retarded, many of whom in the past would have died at an early age. An institution is the only home most of these children will ever know.

The limited abilities of retarded children often lead to the assumption that elaborate facilities are unnecessary and that the environment should merely be durable and easy to clean. The children often spend most of their waking hours in rooms that are surfaced in hard, low-maintenance materials and bare of any contents which can be moved, manipulated, or otherwise affected by the children. Some give up trying to have an effect on their surroundings and spend their day either completely motionless or, alternatively, indulge in endless repetitive behavior, such as rocking back and forth. Others explore every corner of the environment in minute detail: a child may work at loosening a particular screw for months, until his efforts finally meet with success. Nurses must be constantly alert to see that such objects are not swallowed or thrown at other children. These problems are duly noted, and the next institution built is designed to eliminate them — with hidden screws, recessed fittings, sealed windows, seamless floors. The object seems to be an environment in which nothing the child does will have any effect. Soon, even those few children who still harbored some curiosity about the world give up.

The fact that retarded children often have some destructive effect on their environment should be a cause for rejoicing rather than concern, since it represents a heroic effort on their part to deal in some measure with their world. The task of the designer is to provide them with more ways to do what every human being must do to preserve his humanity — to experience life to the fullest degree possible and to have some effect on the world.

One approach might be to construct a series of modular forms of a material (such as foam rubber or styrofoam) that is soft, has a tough surface, and can be cleaned or periodically replaced. These forms would be light to handle and could cause no injury, while providing many possibilities for play. The children could line them up, pile them on top of each other, sit on them, or lie down between them. The floor should also be soft, in order to prevent injuries from falling and to provide a softer and warmer surface to sit or lie on; there are several poured-in-place rubber-like compounds that are resilient and easy to clean.

Alternatively, movable forms could be set into the walls where the children could manipulate them, turn them so different colors appear, and push them back and forth. Lights could flash and bells could ring when buttons were pushed; recessed mirrors could offer views of the children, the sky, and so forth. Similar activities can take place outdoors, where gentle grass mounds and shallow water channels provide additional experience without danger. The important thing is to provide a series of possible activities of varying complexity that allow the children to see the effect

**Sunshine Elementary School Playground: San Diego
James Hubbell, Designer**

Structures of concrete, steel, bronze, glass, and tile in a grassy backyard setting are designed to provide a range of experiences for children who are deaf, blind, or crippled.

their actions can have on their environment.

To conclude this section, the point made previously is offered once again. Experience in human beings is continuous. Some are tragically limited in what they can experience because of physical, mental, or emotional disabilities, but *all* share some part of their experience with all other human beings. Each person, no matter how limited, possesses some measure of intelligence, feeling, and strength. Too often this part of institutionalized persons is not even allowed to develop, much less encouraged. To encourage it is both the limit of what we can do and the full measure of our responsibility to our fellow men.

other opportunities for play

The previous chapters have dealt, for the most part, with the kinds of playgrounds that are built on sites set aside specifically for this purpose, often at some distance from the homes of many persons who use them. These locations have the advantage of sufficient area to serve a large number of children with a comprehensive program, while few nearby residents are disturbed. As important as these playgrounds are, there is also a need for numerous smaller facilities more easily accessible to mothers with young children. Children spend a great deal of time in and around their home, on the block where they live — on the sidewalk or in the street — and in the immediate neighborhood, accompanying their mothers on trips to the market or laundry. Added together, the amount of time spent in close proximity to home and on the daily errands is usually greater than the time available to play in a playground. Play facilities for daily use need not be elaborate or expensive; they could, in fact, be built in during the construction of new buildings, maintenance work on sidewalks, lighting, and fire hydrants, and improvements such as tree-planting, and so on.

Young children spend most of their play time close to home, finding things to do wherever they can. Buildings provide many possibilities for play, although they are usually unintentional.

Properly designed, such facilities could make our streets and sidewalks safer for children and provide a more stimulating and delightful urban environment.

Play in Buildings

A few years ago, a New York corporation began a yearly program of installing a play facility for the Christmas season. Prefabricated units were erected over a heavy, resilient floor matting in the lobby, and mothers were invited to bring their young children. This indoor playground attracted thousands of enthusiastic children and also delighted the adults who worked in the building as well as passers-by. Similarly, a large toy store in New York has provided a long slide leading from a landing of the main stairway to the floor below. The slide is in constant use, competing successfully for the children's attention with all the other toys in the store. These two examples indicate both a need and a means for creating play areas inside public buildings.

The need is particularly great in places where parents and children spend a lot of time, e.g., waiting rooms in airports, bus and train stations, hospitals, municipal buildings, welfare centers, restaurants, and gas stations. The lives of parents and children alike could be made more pleasant if the youngsters could play safely while their parents do errands or simply rest for a few minutes. The next step, of course, is to staff these areas with a trained supervisor, so that children could be left for short periods of time, and this has actually been done in the "check-a-child" playgrounds discussed below.

The most modest place to play near home is often better than a larger space far away. This niche is frequently occupied by one or more children playing a variety of games.

Play on Rooftops and Platforms

Rooftops have been used for play facilities for many years, but few buildings are constructed with adequate roofs for this purpose. As un-built-up land diminishes in our urban centers, rooftops and platforms become increasingly attractive possibilities for the location of play facilities; this represents another aspect of the current trend to make maximum use of urban space by creating layers of different activities. At present, most of the space over highways, railroad tracks, parking lots, and streets is wasted. Platforms usually eliminate much of the noise, fumes, and other dangerous aspects of the areas below, providing ideal locations for residential, educational, and community projects.

Little Red Schoolhouse Playground: New York City
Hammel Green and Abrahamson, Architects

A school rooftop has been developed into an exciting
and varied play space for four- to six-year-olds. The
children can climb, slide, play in sandboxes, or just sit
quietly on the benches. An interesting feature is the use
of sound to help define distinct areas — metallic wind
chimes in the younger children's area (foreground in the
sketch) and deep-toned wooden reeds in the older children's area. Striped awnings give shade and add a colorful touch.

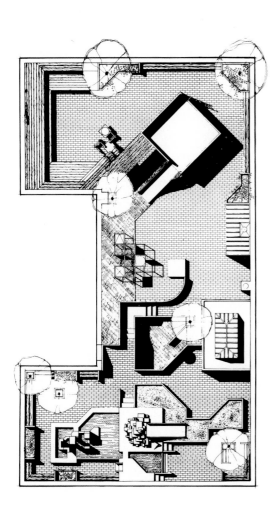

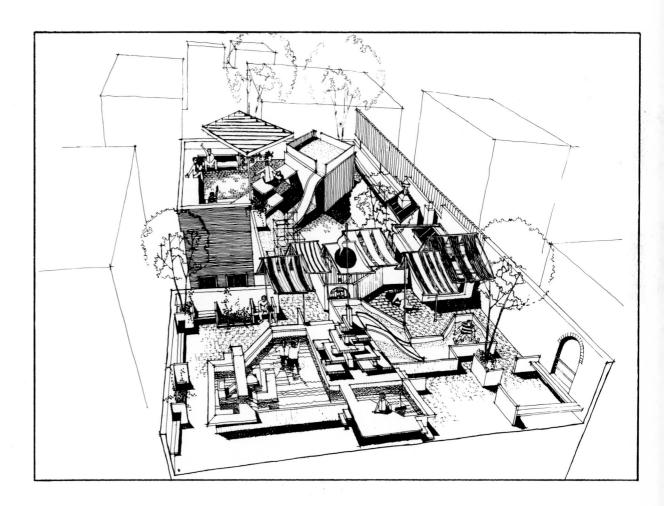

Riverside Park Community: New York City
Richard Dattner, Architect

Shown below is a model of this residential community for 10,000 people that is to be built on a platform over light-industry facilities. Playing fields and playgrounds will be located on platforms over an existing highway and railroad right-of-way.

Platforms in the courtyards (which measure 420 feet in diameter) of two circular apartment houses will roof the parking and traffic levels (opposite page, below, left). On the top level, which is reserved for pedestrians and recreation, are a wading pool (or ice-skating rink), playgrounds for small children, and places for adults to sit.

Reclaimed shorefront can provide many acres of new land for recreation and play facilities. Part of the Community is to be built on filled land in the Hudson River (opposite page, below, right). The design includes a marina and "boatel," an amphitheater, cafes, a restaurant and ballroom, and a variety of play areas related to the waterfront location. A ship will be moored in the marina permanently for children to visit. The structure at left in the drawing encloses the existing highway and forms a platform on which there will be tennis courts and playing fields.

For the designer, the primary considerations in creating platform and rooftop play areas are the construction and materials of the floor surface and the protection of children at the edges. (If the children have any movable equipment that might be thrown or dropped, there is an additional need to protect persons below.) The roof must be enclosed with a material strong enough to withstand normal abuse by children. Play equipment designed for existing buildings must be light enough to be supported by the structure. This usually can be accomplished by using wood or plastics and making the base wide enough to distribute the weight of the piece over a large area. Water should be limited to sprays or showers, since the weight of a deep pool usually cannot be borne by a roof that was not specifically designed for the purpose. A particularly heavy element can sometimes be located over a column, depending on the structure of the building. An architect or structural engineer should always be consulted before changes are made or structures are added to an existing building.

New buildings, of course, can be designed to accommodate any kind of play facility, including swimming and wading pools, sand pits, and

Promenade Apartments Deck: Riverdale, New York City
Richard Dattner, Architect

A steel and concrete recreation deck (right) covers several levels of parking as well as railroad tracks that pass under a cooperative housing development. Planting and shade trellises enclose promenades, a tennis court, a small wading pool, and play areas for toddlers.

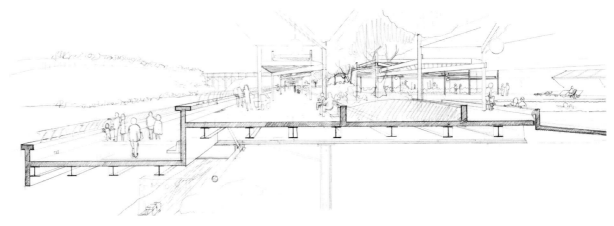

With some minor modifications, many buildings could be used for many kinds of play, including basketball or even finger painting. Warehouses and factories, for example, often have few windows and require only loading docks at ground level — the rest of the wall space is fine material for creating play areas.

planted areas. Some additional cost is involved because of the increased load capacity required, and the surface materials, which must allow for heavy use in addition to their usual waterproofing function. Fencing also adds to the cost, but all the extra expense amounts to a fraction of the value of an equivalent piece of property.

Play with Buildings

As any child knows but adults seldom remember, almost any building creates opportunities for play. There are steps to jump from, walls to hit balls against, railings to slide down, fire escapes to swing from or use for basketball games (the lowest rung of the raised ladder makes the basket), and ledges to climb along. Modern architecture is often too monolithic and smooth-surfaced to offer possibilities for much besides graffitti-painting or window-breaking: vandalism may always be with us, but imaginatively designed buildings might provide enough alternatives to vandalism to materially decrease its appeal.

Among the items that can easily be built into new buildings are: recessed blackboards (it is cheaper for the management to provide chalk

Garden Street Tot Lot: New Haven
New Haven Redevelopment Agency
Arthur Selbert, Designer

Simple forms set into walls are inexpensive and can provide entertaining experience for youngsters.

Children have long since discovered the possibilities for play inherent in urban "street furniture."

than to remove ink and spray paint); movable (but not removable) colored blocks and spheres set into walls so they can be rearranged in different patterns; bits of mirrors or other shiny materials, both flat and distorted, in which children can see their reflections; objects that produce interesting sounds of low volume when struck; colored tiles, seashells, and impressions made by mechanical parts and other forms cast into the concrete at an appropriate height (most adults would not even notice these); slides adjacent to entrance stairs; brass sliding poles extending from low platforms to the ground, and so on. Many other ideas will appear during the planning of a specific project; as with any design for play, the most important thing is to create a variety of interesting experiences that can in some way be controlled by the children.

Play on Sidewalks

City sidewalks possess a potential for play that has not been fully exploited by designers, although children have already discovered uses for the raw materials offered by these areas. By redesigning some common features, most of the problems inherent in sidewalk play can be eliminated.

A proposal for utilizing sidewalk and street space that is usually wasted to create small "play nodes" in residential areas. The sidewalks are widened at intersections and at fire hydrants in the middle of the block, where parking is prohibited. The paving between the curbs is painted in bright stripes to alert motorists. This kind of play area serves a number of functions, does not require buying costly land, is indestructible and safe, and is inexpensive enough to be built on almost every block in a city.

Low concrete benches form a protected area, shaded by trees, where mothers can sit while the children play. (The benches should be high enough to prevent infants from climbing over.) Sand is used within the areas ringed by benches, brick in the space between them.

Modifications of the curb, which forms the boundary between the street and the sidewalk, would greatly increase the possibilities for safe play. The curb around fire hydrants should be partially extended into the street and raised a few feet in height. This would utilize the space currently wasted in the street (and simplify the enforcement of parking prohibitions) for additional sidewalk play space, while discouraging children from running into the street. Children who want to cross the street will be able to see the traffic, and themselves be seen before crossing. With a little change in the design of the hydrant itself, a small sitting and play area could be created at intervals on every block. A different paving material and a tree or two can make this an attractive — and inexpensive — facility for mothers with baby carriages in the daytime and adults and teenagers in the afternoon and evening. (Checker tables can be furnished at a small additional cost.)

One of the simplest and least expensive possibilities is to cast lines and squares for a variety of games into sidewalk paving; interesting forms can be impressed or objects embedded in it; and even different textures are noticed by

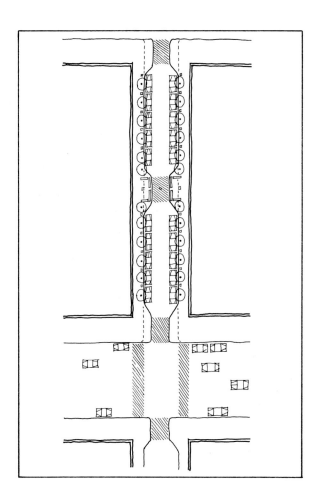

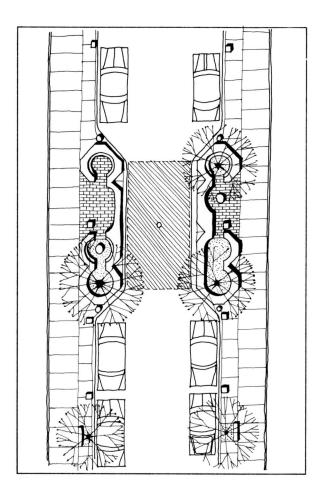

In warm weather, the area might be chained off and through traffic eliminated; vehicles could make U-turns in the space on either side of the play area. The water spray in the street (see sketch) is connected to the fire hydrants, which have been redesigned in a cube shape so that children can sit on them. The parking meters too are cube-shaped, thus providing the seating so lacking in American cities (but, unlike the standard park benches, not providing a place to sleep). New lighting fixtures also make the play nodes pleasant places for adults to sit on warm evenings.

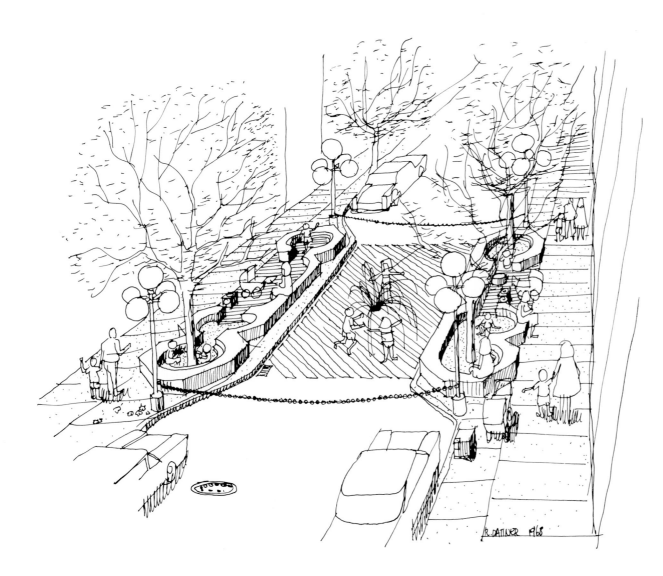

children who, being much closer to the ground than adults, are very sensitive to the surface they walk on.

In Cumbernauld, a new city in Scotland, a double row of cobblestones set into the main pedestrian walks indicates a route that leads to the center of the city without crossing a single road. The pedestrian walks of Cumbernauld also provide widened places, surfaced in cobblestones or dirt, that serve as play areas. These spots are small and simple in design, but their location near homes and away from traffic makes them a valuable complement to other, larger playgrounds.

The possibilities for sidewalk play areas are inexhaustible: where trees are planted, on mailboxes, in the design of waste receptacles, street signs, and even manhole covers, which could be made suitable for games with marbles. Lampposts can support basketball hoops or volley-ball nets in areas where streets are closed off for play. The construction of any sidewalk and its ancillary utilities represents a large capital outlay, and to use the space fully is economical rather than the reverse.

Play Facility: Cumbernauld New Town, Scotland

A colorful mural and four sections of concrete pipe create a small play area along a pedestrian path.

Playground: Cumbernauld New Town, Scotland

At a safe distance from vehicular traffic, this simple arrangement gives children a place to play right next to home. Such areas are very effective if used in conjunction with larger playgrounds in the neighborhood.

Playground: Cumbernauld New Town, Scotland

These gently inclined cobblestone mounds are not only fun for the children, but they also make an attractive landscape. The large mound is high enough to contain sand effectively, while it is not hard to climb even for the youngest children. All traffic has been kept on the other side of the dwellings.

Plaza Fountain: Reston, Virginia
Conklin & Rossant, Architects

In one of the first "new towns" in the United States, a combination fountain and play facility gives life and a sense of activity to an urban space. The wading pool is formed by a rise in the brick pavement. As in Cumbernauld, all traffic is carefully located away from the pedestrian paths.

Play Sculpture and Lookout Tower: Reston, Virginia
Conklin & Rossant, Architects
Gonzalo Fonseca, Sculptor

To visually emphasize this turn in one of the major pedestrian routes to the commercial area, the designers have created a concrete landscape, with a boat-shaped pit filled with sand.

Play Construction: Reston, Virginia
Gonzalo Fonseca, Sculptor

This structure can be appreciated not only as a miniature playground but also as a work of art.

Play Street Project: New York City
Michael Altschuler, Designer

Plan for a play street used in conjunction with a store-front. The storefront provides storage for play and construction materials, office space for supervisory staff, and indoor play facilities in bad weather.

In the second sketch, a lamppost is equipped with a basketball hoop. Street furniture can be used for a variety of play equipment: a volleyball net, for example, might be suspended between two lampposts.

Play on Streets

The play potential of city streets has already been demonstrated — in New York City, for example, the Police Athletic League operates programs in many streets closed off for play at stated times. Activities include volley ball, basketball, music programs, and storytelling, and fire hydrants are sometimes fitted with sprays for water play. But the major lack is in activities for very young children, who need protected areas where they can play with sand and water; one solution to this problem is mobile or prefabricated playgrounds that can be transported to a closed street and set up quickly.

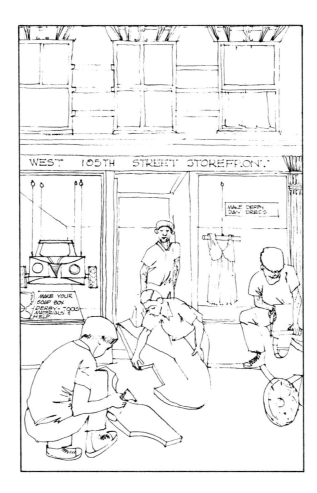

Police Athletic League Play Street: New York City

Every summer, the Police Athletic League of New York City runs scores of play streets. Although the equipment is rudimentary, the program is successful because it offers activities supervised by a trained and enthusiastic staff.

Sprinkler heads, which conserve water and do not reduce water pressure in fire hydrants, are provided by the New York Police Department.

Prefabricated Playground: Playstreet Incorporated
Richard Dattner, Architect

These modular units are made of strong reinforced
plastic and can be used indoors or out. Light in weight,
they do not require expensive foundations. The joining
system allows the units to be assembled in any number
of combinations, depending on how many units are used
and the location and size of the site.

Vest-Pocket Playground: New York City
M. Paul Friedberg, Landscape Architect

An interesting and attractive play area replacing several vacant lots, this facility nevertheless suffers from a lack of regular maintenance, as do many vest-pocket playgrounds.

Vest-Pocket Playground: New York City
M. Paul Friedberg, Landscape Architect

Plastic-covered cables held by a sturdy frame make a structure that is both safe and fun to bounce on. It is located in a lot between two buildings.

"Vest-Pocket" Playgrounds

"Vest-pocket" playgrounds are usually built on small vacant lots and equipped with a variety of play structures as well as seating for adults. Most of them share problems that seem unrelated to the success of the design but apparently stem from the in-between nature of the facility.

The location of vest-pocket playgrounds out of sight of most street traffic encourages night-time use by derelicts and the accumulation of trash. Their small size limits the number of activities possible and makes a full-time supervisor uneconomical; without a supervised program, children may tire of the place and go back to the street, and disuse invites deterioration and vandalism. Maintenance and responsibility for what happens is obviously a considerably greater problem with a number of small facilities than with one large facility.

The small sidewalk sitting and play areas discussed earlier need no extra maintenance or supervision because they are already on the route of sanitation departments, and they are informally supervised by everyone in the vicin-

133

A vest-pocket park without supervisors or clearly established responsibilities for upkeep can become a teen-age trysting place, derelict hotel, or just plain garbage heap.

ity. Large playgrounds provide enough activities to keep children involved for long periods of time, while maintenance and full-time supervision become economical. The vest-pocket playground falls in between. Three vest-pocket playgrounds that cost $35,000 each will serve only a fraction of the children accommodated in one $100,000 playground, and provide a much smaller selection of possible activities. Their main advantages are accessibility and the fact that small vacant lots are usually more plentiful than large ones.

One kind of small park-playground — those operated by and adjacent to nursery schools and kindergartens — seems to work, and this suggests that under certain conditions the vest-pocket idea can be successful, and a much-used and valuable asset to the community. First, the responsibility for their operation and maintenance must be well defined. School, church, and community organizations take full responsibility for every aspect of attached play facilities. Their insurance protects the users, and their employees supervise and maintain the area. The persons who are responsible are readily available, unlike the vast, distant, and overworked city agency.

Next, a program of activities must be provided. The use of the play facility is broadened if there is a planned program and trained personnel to direct it. Equipment can be distributed when needed and put away when not in use, and organized activities such as storytelling and painting are possible.

Finally, use of the facility must be controlled. The children using the playground of an organization are known to the staff, who can close and lock the playground at night and when supervision is not available.

Activity-oriented Playgrounds

Life in a city is fascinating, and all the resources of the city should be used to create playgrounds in which children can expand their range of experience. For example, a waterfront playground could be equipped with a real boat, cargo nets, ropes, and pulleys; other playgrounds could be constructed around airplanes, railroads, theater, construction, printing, sewing — almost any activity that utilizes special equipment or processes; such playgrounds might be run by trade organizations.

Check-a-Child Playground: New York City
Richard Dattner, Architect

This facility was built next to an old band shell in an area with many stores; for a small fee, many parents can "check" their children here while they shop. Simple wood structures were combined with commercially produced climbing equipment to keep the cost of the facility low. The pavement is covered with rubber safety surfacing. Slides leading from the two towers and the building to the sandboxes were added later. Picnic tables (against two walls) are used for games, and trained supervisors organize a variety of activities to keep the children occupied.

"Check-a-Child" Playgrounds

A prototype "check-a-child" playground, financed by an association of retail stores, has been built in a New York City park. At this playground parents may deposit children for a few hours for a nominal charge. Age limits prevent parents from leaving children too young to be without their mothers or too old to be supervised easily. Each child receives a numbered tag and the parents a numbered check, with which they reclaim the child. (Any child unclaimed by 4:00 P.M., the daily closing time, is taken to a nearby police station to await his parents.) A mother may thus do her shopping or other errands while her child is in the care of trained supervisors, and the service is inexpensive enough to be used by those who cannot afford a private baby-sitter. After hours and on weekends the playground is open for public, unsupervised use.

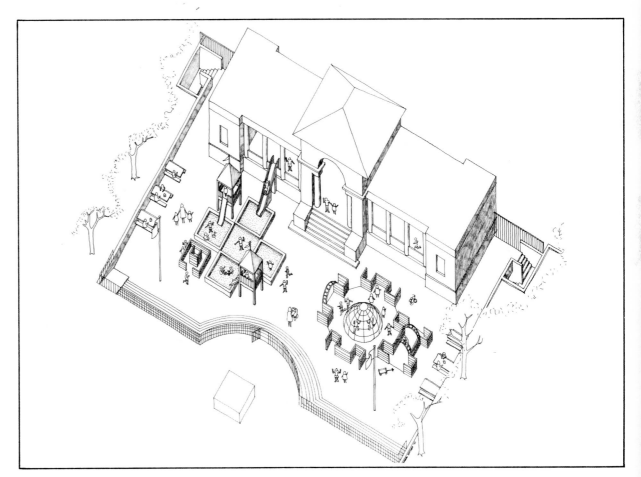

Highbridge Funicular: New York City
Richard Dattner, Architect

As illustrated by the sketch (right), many unused stretches of waterfront might be made accessible by devices such as the funicular, and the areas used for floating recreation facilities.

Harlem River Recreation Area: New York City
Richard Dattner, Architect

Surplus barges can be converted into floating swimming pools, playgrounds, cafés, and discothèques — all these actually exist in Rome and Paris.

Playgrounds on Barges

The problem of finding suitable space for the construction of new play facilities leads to the consideration of playgrounds that could float on the waterways near which many cities are built. Surplus barges are available from railroad and shipping companies at low prices, and with renovation they provide a large area that can be taken to different locations as needed. A typical barge is about 30 by 120 feet, with room below deck for storage and portable toilets. They can be used by teenagers for dances, parties, and films in the evening without disturbing surrounding residents. A major playground can be created by linking together a number of barges containing a variety of facilities, from sandboxes to basketball courts and swimming pools. The construction would be completed in a boatyard, and the barge delivered to its berth complete. Such a playground might be kept in one location while a permanent playground is under construction; upon completion of the new facility, the barge could be moved to a new location, marking the beginning of work on another new facility.

Park Barge: New York City
Richard Dattner, Architect

This compact floating recreation facility includes climbing towers and slides for children and an amphitheater for live performances or films. A translucent screen allows people on the shore to see the films, and there are loudspeakers to amplify the sound for a large audience. A snack bar with tables and chairs can become a dance floor by night. Public toilets and storage space for extra seating are below deck.

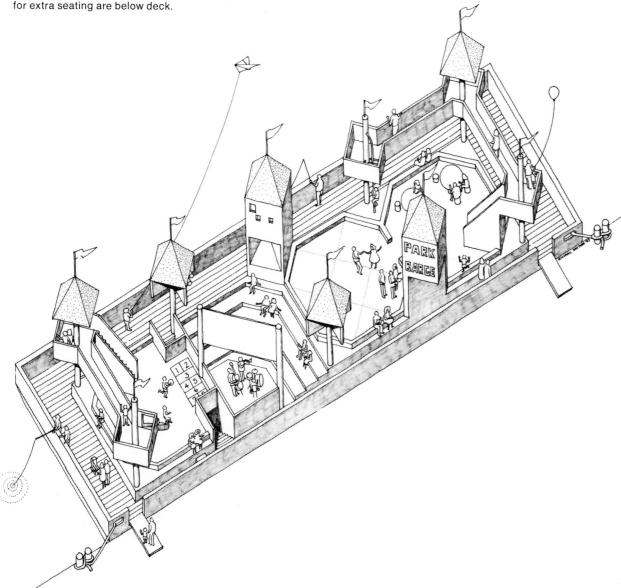

Conclusion

Play is the way that children learn about themselves and the world they live in. In the process of mastering familiar situations and learning to cope with new ones, their intelligence and personality grow, as well as their bodies. The environment for play must be rich in experience, and it must be, to a significant extent, under the control of the child. It must allow each child to exercise choice and to grow, safely, at his own rate.

If these qualities are present, environments for play can be created almost anywhere — in parks or streets, on sidewalks, rooftops, or barges. If they are not, the most elaborate facility will be sterile and unused.

In this book many different playgrounds have been presented; all have as their goal the creation of an environment where play, learning, and the human spirit are nurtured. Design is also a form of play, and these designs are offered to the reader as the experiments of designers, not as complete solutions. If they are successful, it is to the extent that the designers have listened to that which is playful in children, and in themselves.

comparative dimensions of children

Age 2

Boys		Girls	
34	height	33.7	height

Age 4

40.9	height	40.9	height
38	weight	37	weight
16.7	arm reach	16.4	arm reach
9.5	chair height	10	chair height

Age 6

Boys		Girls	
46.1	height	45.8	height
48	weight	46	weight
18.8	arm reach	18.9	arm reach
11.6	chair height	11	chair height

Age 8

Boys		Girls	
50.4	height	50	height
58	weight	57	weight
21.5	arm reach	21.2	arm reach
13	chair height	12.5	chair height

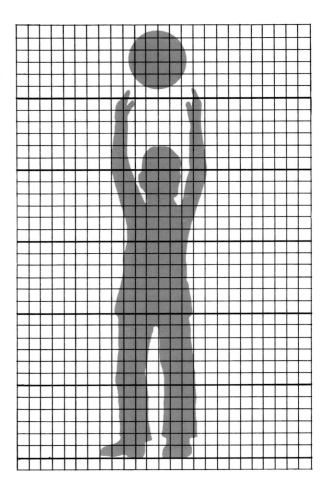

Measurements given in inches.   Dimensions based on *The Measure of Man: Human Factors in Design*, by Henry Dreyfuss.

Age 10

Boys

54.3	height
71	weight
23.4	arm reach
14	chair height

Girls

54.2	height
70	weight
23.3	arm reach
13	chair height

Age 12

Boys

58.2	height
86	weight
25.3	arm reach
14.5	chair height

Girls

59	height
90	weight
25.7	arm reach
14.7	chair height

Age 14

Boys

63	height
109	weight
27.9	arm reach
16	chair height

Girls

62.3	height
108	weight
27.3	arm reach
15	chair height

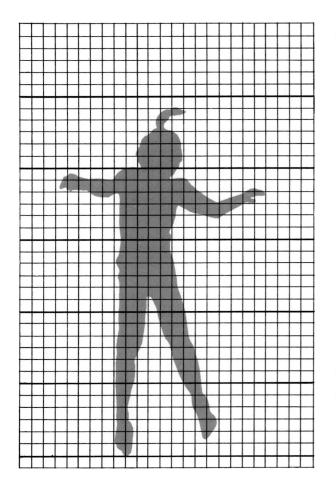

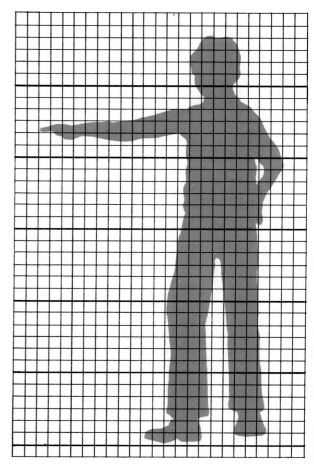

bibliography

* Paperback

Lady Allen of Hurtwood. *New Playgrounds.* London: The Housing Centre, 1964. (Pamphlet)

———. *Planning for Play.* London: Thames and Hudson, 1968.

———. *Play Parks.* London: The Housing Centre, 1964. (Pamphlet)

Lady Allen of Hurtwood, *et al. Play in Hospital.* London: World Organization for Early Childhood Education (OMEP), 1966. (Pamphlet)

———. *Space for Play.* Copenhagen: World Organization for Early Childhood Education (OMEP), 1964. (Pamphlet)

———. *Two to Five in High Flats.* London: The Housing Centre, 1961. (Pamphlet)

Ariès, Phillipe. *Centuries of Childhood.* New York: Vintage Books, 1962.*

Bettelheim, Bruno. *The Empty Fortress.* New York: The Free Press, 1967.

Dreyfuss, Henry. *The Measure of Man: Human Factors in Design.* New York: Whitney Publications, 1967.

Erikson, Erik H. *Childhood and Society.* New York: W.W. Norton & Co., 1963.*

———. *The Challenge of Youth.* New York: Anchor Books, 1965.*

Frank, Lawrence K. *On the Importance of Infancy.* New York: Random House, 1966.*

Haimowitz, Morris and Natalie. *Human Development.* New York: Thomas Y. Crowell, 1966.*

Huizinga, Johan. *Homo Ludens.* Boston: Beacon Press, 1966.*

Jacobs, Jane. *The Death and Life of Great American Cities.* New York: Random House, 1961.*

Laing, Ronald D. *The Bird of Paradise* and *The Politics of Experience.* Harmondsworth: Penguin Books, 1967.*

———. *The Divided Self.* London: Pelican Books, 1965.*

Ledermann, A., and Traschel, A. *Creative Playgrounds and Recreational Places.* Rev. ed. New York: Frederick A. Praeger, 1968.

Lowenfeld, Margaret. *Play in Childhood.* New York: John Wiley, 1967.*

Mead, Margaret, and Wolfenstein, Martha. *Childhood in Contemporary Cultures.* Chicago: University of Chicago Press, 1955.

Mussen, Paul H. *The Psychological Development of the Child.* Englewood Cliffs, New Jersey: Prentice Hall, 1963.*

Muuss, Rolf E. *Theories of Adolescence.* New York: Random House, 1962.*

Piaget, Jean. *Play, Dreams and Imitation in Childhood.* New York: W.W. Norton & Co., 1962.*

Rosenblith, Judy F., and Allinsmith, Wesley. *The Causes of Behavior.* Boston: Allyn and Bacon, 1962.*

Stone, Joseph L., and Church, Joseph. *Childhood and Adolescence.* New York: Random House, 1957.

acknowledgments

I would like to thank the following individuals, organizations, and agencies for their part in creating the play environments described in this book:

The Parks, Recreation and Cultural Affairs Administration of New York City: August Heckscher, Administrator; William R. Ginsberg, Deputy Administrator; Elliot Willensky, Deputy Administrator for Design; Victor Losco, Director of Design; also Thomas P. F. Hoving, former Administrator; Peter Aschkenasy, former Deputy Administrator; and Arthur Rosenblatt, former Director of Design.

The Honorable John V. Lindsay, Mayor of New York, whose administration actively encouraged innovation in playground design.

The Committee for a Creative Playground: Clare Beckhardt, Diane Ravitch, and Sue Mellins, former Directors.

The Estée and Joseph Lauder Foundation, and Leonard and Evelyn Lauder, for their major role in shaping the Adventure Playground.

Dr. and Mrs. Herman Harris and Steven Selig, and their friends, who donated the Lower Playground in memory of Judith Harris Selig, Laura Ross Selig, and Pamela Kate Selig.

Mr. and Mrs. Robert Weintraub, donors of the improvements to the West 81st Street Playground.

The Heckscher Foundation for Children, Mrs. Arthur Smadbeck, President, donor of the Heckscher Playground.

The Louis and Bessie Adler Foundation, donor of the East 72nd Street Playground.

The 14th Street Association, donor of the Union Square Check-a-Child Playground.

The staff of the Children's Rehabilitation Unit, Bird S. Coler Hospital.

The Children's Day Treatment Center.

Riverdale Neighborhood House.

The Negro Labor Committee, sponsor of Riverside Park Community.

Grayco Builders, developer of Riverside Park Community and Promenade Apartments.

Union Free School District #13, Valley Stream, New York.

I would like also to thank the many persons, too numerous to mention, with whom I spoke or corresponded while writing Design for Play. The assistance, advice, and material received from them helped make this book a reality.

Special thanks are due Nancy C. Newman, for her editorial assistance.

Finally, I am grateful to my wife, Shelly, for her help throughout the writing of this book, but especially in the sections dealing with the psychology of play.

picture credits

Boldface indicates page number; credits are given from left to right.

index

Drawing by Barney Tobey. Copyright 1966, The New
Yorker Magazine, Inc.

"Damn it, they don't have swings in here!"